Theology Today:

18 Theology and Spirituality

Theology Today

GENERAL EDITOR:

EDWARD YARNOLD, S.J.

No. 18

Theology and Spirituality

BY

JOHN DALRYMPLE

distributed by
CLERGY BOOK SERVICE
HALES CORNERS, WISCONSIN

Nihil Obstat:
Jeremiah J. O'Sullivan, D.D.,
Censor deputatus
14th May 1970

Imprimatur:
Cornelius Ep. Corcag. & Ross
25th May 1970

ISBN 0-85342-244-9

CONTENTS

PREFACE

Many books have been written describing the normal course of progress in prayer and giving practical help for this ascent of Mount Carmel. There have been many works on Christian living, like the great classics by a Kempis, St Francis of Sales and Alphonsus Rodriguez. But books about the *theology* of prayer and Christian living have been much rarer. We write about theology and we write about prayer; but what is the connection between our theology and our ascetical and spiritual teaching? Father Dalrymple makes the connection. After investigating the theological principles, he goes on to examine the normal course of Christian progress – not in the abstract, but in the contemporary world.

E. J. Yarnold, S.J.

ACKNOWLEDGEMENTS

The scriptural quotations in this publication are from the *Revised Standard Version of the Bible* copyrighted 1946 and 1952 by the Division of Christian Education of the National Council of the Churches of Christ in the U.S.A. and used by permission. W. B. Yeats's poem *The Indian upon God* is quoted by permission of Mr M. B. Yeats, MacMillan and Co. Ltd. (London). Dr W. E. Orchard's autobiography is quoted by permission of Putnam and Co. Ltd. (London). To all of these we offer our grateful thanks.

AUTHOR'S NOTE

The plan of this book is that first of all we examine how the doctrinal facts of Christian revelation affect Christian spirituality (Part I). Next we investigate the elements of this spirituality in so far as it is a response to revelation (Part II). Finally we examine how the elements of Christian spirituality develop in the personal spiritual growth of the individual (Part III). Parts I and II are concerned with a movement from the outside inwards; this is necessary because Christianity is a religion of revelation. Part III is concerned with a movement from the inside outwards; this is necessary because Christianity is a way of life and therefore must be personally authentic.

PART I

The Christian Response

1. The Presence of God in the World

Religion is the meeting point between God and man. It is the commerce that goes on between them, their mutual presence. It takes place in this world because God is present in this world and it is there that he meets man. God is not remote from his creation, but is dynamically present in it as the creating force keeping it in being. He is the ground of our being, the ontological atmosphere which we breathe and in which we are immersed. The Greek philosophers in their attempt to portray the absolute transcendence of God produced a model for men's imaginations which pictured him as a remote and static Being above and beyond the fleeting world.

This is not a good model for the Reality we are trying to portray, because God is not remote from the world but present in every particle of matter in it. He is present in every one of this world's realities, in terrible events like wars and earthquakes, but also in the vein of a flower and the wing of a fly, because he is the sustaining force keeping all in being. Above all God is present in persons and their relationships to each other, for they are the nearest approach to him in creation. We must not, then, think of a God whose 'activity' is in this world but whose 'essence' is somehow apart in a remote and static heaven. Rather we have to remember that in God his rest and activity are all one and consequently God himself is immersed in the here and now. He is the Ultimate Reality of our everyday lives, in him we live and move and have our being. This nearness of God to everyday life is of course quite compatible with his transcendence and utter unknowability. It merely brings home to us the fact that the mystery of God is part and parcel with our lives and not locked away in a separate compartment apart from daily living, or in 'heaven'. The mystery of God and the mystery of life in this world are in fact two aspects of one and the same thing.

A further feature of God's presence in the world is that it is a personal presence. God, whose presence is encountered everywhere, is not an impersonal force or field, exercising an impersonal influence upon men and events. His omnipresent influence is supremely personal. He has in fact revealed himself to men as a person. To say bluntly that God is *a* person is to make difficulties for many today. They are able to think of God as the divine field of force in which we exist, and are ready to concede that this force is personal, but they do not allow that God is *a* person, an object 'out there', separate from the world. We will deal with this problem in the next chapter. Here let it suffice to say that to call God a person is not to tie oneself down to a world picture which involves a God out there, separate from the world he creates. It is merely to use one of the models given to us for God (the most frequent one in the New Testament) alongside others, with which to build a comprehensive spirituality. It should be remembered that no one idea or image for God is sufficient for plumbing the depths of the truth about him, and that the only way to do so is to remember that all the models we have for God are limited and inadequate, so that it is good to have more than one even if they appear to contradict each other. In much the same way scientific progress often depends on having more than one 'contradictory' model for nature, like the wave theory and particle theory of matter. Especially in this matter of models for God there is safety in numbers. They complement and counteract each other.

Since we can call God a person, then, it is fruitful to ponder upon how persons are present to each other. They are able to be 'present' to one another in a far deeper and more intense way than animals and inanimate things can. They are mutually present by penetrating each other in knowledge and love, and by acting and reacting spiritually towards each other in a way that admits of growth and diminishment, in all the degrees from cold recognition to close intimacy. For instance, lovers meeting for the hundredth time and two strangers sitting opposite each other in a railway train are both present to each other, but the former far *more so* than the latter. It is the same with God and man. Religion is their mutual presence, and like the mutual presence of two human beings, it can vary in intensity on man's part from purely formal recognition to burning ardour. Primarily, then, religion is a state of being, the intangible but very real state of relationship that exists between a man and God. This presence is bound up with what the man believes about God (creed), how he responds to God (cult) and how he behaves as a result (code), but these three are only expressions of the much deeper and more primary fact that he is relating to God and God to him. It is, of course, an unequal relationship, and deeply mysterious, not only because men and women are deeply mysterious in their relationships, but above all because God is Mystery beyond human comprehension.

The active presence of God in the world has other features which bear upon religion and determine its nature. (Theologians distinguish two activities of God in this world, viz. Creation and Redemption, but warn us not to treat them as if they were separate actions. For our purposes we can regard them as one active presence of God to us, recognising the distinction between nature and grace without going further into it.) First of all, God's presence to men is purely the initiative of God and utterly gratuitous. God preexists. He keeps all men in existence. He sustains not only the man who believes in him but the atheist and agnostic too. They do not advert to the fact that they are depending on God for their being, but they are. God makes men. The only sense in which men 'make' God is the epistemological sense: they grope towards and stumble upon him already existing and then create a concept of him in their minds. What we call the Redemption is equally gratuitous. The initiative, in both the Old and New testaments, rests entirely with God. He approached men, calling the Israelites from ignorance and unbelief to a destiny which was entirely his plan, his covenant. This in turn blossomed into the Incarnation, God's supreme initiative towards men. The story of the Bible is not the story of man's quest for God but the far more astonishing story of God's quest for man. From this divine initiative it follows that the life of man is entirely a gift from God. Man did not have to exist or be redeemed! God is under no obligation to create or to redeem. Every creature exists because of God's free and undetermined choice. The message of the Bible, as opposed to that of the philosophers, is that God creates and redeems man by a free and gratuitous act, which is pure bounty.

Secondly, God's active presence to men is continuous and immanent. These two qualities can be said to be the 'earthly' qualities of God's presence to us. The fact that God creates and redeems gratuitously and of his own initiative establishes for us that he is a 'heavenly' God, but the fact that this divine initiative is all the time within us, throbbing through the world like the engines of a great ship, brings home that God is also earthly, very much part of this world, not remote from it. This immanent activity of God in the world has to be recognised as a living thing, a personal divine presence to each individual by the power of creation and, in baptised persons, the living presence of the Trinity. 'We will come to him and make our home with him' (Jn 14.23). It is a continuous and immanent Presence.

The response man makes to this active presence of God to him is his religion, and from our brief analysis of this divine presence as originating from God and immanent to man we can see two fundamental features of Christianity. First of all, it is a *response.* The Christian religion is not the result of men approaching God and working out a religion from their experience, but the opposite. It is the result of God approaching men (first through the patriarchs and prophets, then ultimately in Christ, the Son) and men reacting to that approach. The Christian religion is not an initiating action of man but a reaction on man's part to the advance of God. The image we should have of Christian spirituality is of God pursuing men with his love (which makes demands) and his mercy. However much it may at times seem so, we should not encourage the image of ourselves pursuing a retreating and elusive God. The opposite is truer to the revealed facts. It is God who is doing the pursuing and men who so often are running away. Christianity is not so much men speaking to God and trying to make him listen, as men listening to an ever present God and trying to obey. This means that there are two elements which are basic to Christian spirituality: the element of *adoration,* or recognition of a God who exists without our help and creates us, and the element of *thanksgiving* to a God who shares his divine life with us for no other reason than sheer bounty. In other words, because God's creation and redemption are bounteous acts, the two elements of adoration and eucharist (thanksgiving) are primary in Christianity. They are the simple recognition of what God is and does. To omit them or place them second to Christian action is to miss the point of Christianity. Christianity demands action, but it must be action which springs from and itself is adoration and eucharist.

Secondly, we saw that God's active presence in the world was immanent to man, a life within him; not merely an extrinsic and awesome external fact but a divine presence within. This means that the Christian religion is not only a matter of adoration and thanksgiving of the transcendent Saviour, but is also a *life* lived with and in him. Furthermore this immanent divine life is continuous and bound up with the whole of a man's life, not with parts of it. The Christian religion is not one which can be confined to episodes in man's life, episodes of worship and 'religion', but is a special dimension to the whole of living. God and the Christian Fact are present all the time and in the whole of life, and therefore man's response to this, which is Christian spirituality, is also something which is in the whole of life and not a separate part which can be confined to distinct times and places. There are in fact no gaps in life into which Christianity can be deflected, but Christianity is itself the whole of life, or rather a special dimension to human life, a way of living which affects everything a man does and thinks, because it is a special relationship to this world as well as to God. It is a commerce between man in the world, and God the Father, Son and Holy Ghost, which is continual (and therefore inescapable) and of God's choosing (and therefore not optional). The purpose of this book is to examine this commerce between God and men more closely. This preliminary chapter has been merely to establish that Christian spirituality is a response and a life, because the God who reveals himself to men in Christ is a God who is present to man as his Creator and Redeemer, and intimately united to him as his Life.

2. *God and the Fundamental Religious Experience*

If the first experience of God is that he is present to men as the ultimate meaning of life, then the second insight is the realisation that he is a hidden God completely beyond the powers of man to comprehend. The basic paradox of all religion is in fact this contradictory situation that we know God to be the very element in which we live and move and have our being, nearer to the core of our self than ourselves, but when we try to grasp who and what God is he eludes us and seems far away. God eludes us precisely because he is God and beyond the power of man to define by conceptualisation. The Bible itself bears witness to this paradox. No people were more conscious of the nearness of God to their lives than the Jews, but they jealously preserved the tradition that for all his nearness God is somehow 'beyond', not in a spatial sense because he dwells with his people, but in terms of their trying to understand him. He is a hidden God (Is 45.15), whose ways are not man's ways but far above them (Is 55.8-9), who cannot be seen face to face but only in the back (Exod 33.17-23), who can never be represented by any image and to see whom is to die. Even the Incarnation of the Son of God, which brought God nearer to men than ever before, at the same time served to emphasize the far-away-ness of God who 'dwells in unapproachable light, whom no man has ever seen or can see' (1 Tim 6.16) and who can only be discerned in this life 'in a mirror dimly' (1 Cor 13.12), for men walk by faith and have to wait for their glorification for the reward of seeing him face to face. The paradox remains, then, even after the Incarnation, that God is closer to us than anyone in the sense of being the ground of our being and source of our life, but further away than anyone in the sense of being incomprehensible. The tension of religion lies in grasping both these truths and keeping them together, while the temptation (which must be resisted because it does disservice to the truth) is to choose either one or the other rather than both: either to emphasise the nearness of God and in doing so subtly limit him and make him to the image and likeness of man, a 'super' sort of human father or scientific force, or to overemphasise the transcendence of

God and so exile him to heaven safely away from life in this world. In the last chapter we emphasised the nearness of God to man. In this chapter we examine the other aspect, the 'far-away-ness' of God, because it is equally fundamental to religion and to forget it is to distort the truth.

What is being taught by the Bible in the passages alluded to above is the truth that because God is infinite, a man's finite mind can neither imagine him nor conceive him. Clearly no image (a material thing whether in the mind or out of it) can truly portray God, who is infinite Spirit. But no spiritual concept can adequately portray God either, because all concepts in our minds are forged from our experience (which is directly of finite things) and are necessarily therefore finite representations. But God is infinite; hence when we do form ideas of God they are produced as finite, limited ideas which are infinitely inadequate to represent the Reality they are trying to represent. In other words, try as we may, there is always an infinite gap between any model we have of God and God himself. This is true of all the models which we have of God, not only of some. Broadly speaking, there are three types of model we use for trying to represent God to ourselves and others. There are the frankly figurative ones, as when the psalmist calls God his refuge or his rock. There are the personal models of the Old and New testaments – God as Father, Shepherd, Judge, King, etc. And there are the philosophical models: God as Ground of our Being, Divine Field of Force, Ultimate Reality, Supreme Spirit, etc. These models are all necessary at various times in the spiritual life and each expresses a truth about God. The important thing is to remember that they are not ideas *of* God, but only infinitely inadequate human pictures. In fact when we think about God we can be certain of one thing only; what we end up with in our minds is an idea of not-God. In 'finding' God we have lost him. *Un dieu défini est un dieu fini.* This is the paradox.

It is one thing to read what has been said above and give assent to it. It is another to experience it. The fundamental religious experience (common to all higher religions) is the felt experience of that infinite gap between the ideas we have of God and God himself. Philosophers know this to be so, but the mystics feel it, for they have come up against it painfully in their attempts to contact God. At the end of every avenue to God from man, whether he starts from his own experience of life or some sacred book or rite, there lies this infinite gap, a frustrating reminder in practice of the transcendence of God. From this experience, which is primarily a thing to be felt but which can be verified intellectually, we can conclude that there are two forms of the knowledge of God. These can be called positive and negative theology, taking theology in its broad sense to mean the living knowledge of God rather than the academic study of him.

Positive theology or knowledge of God is the kind we have by taking what we know about God in human terms and correlating it all together, so building up a corpus of knowledge about God and his revelation which we call our Theology. It consists of affirmations about God. It is important that the knowledge we thus have of God be expressed in relevant and living concepts, taking its language from the centre of contemporary culture and asking the questions about God and this world which contemporary men ask. Clearly also it must use the revelation of God in the Bible and the Church as its source. In this way the Church in its history drew out of the original revelation the notions of person, nature, grace, with which to explain God, giving us the dogmas of our religion like the Trinity, the Incarnation, the Sacraments, these being no more than the original message of the gospel understood in terms of a later European culture. This process of expressing the gospel in contemporary terms is going on with renewed urgency in our own day. The secularisation of culture and religion is giving rise to new models for the relationship between God and men, as we saw in Chapter 1. They are models which suit the mind and temperament of 'man come of age' better. They are the latest form of affirmative theology, which must always be evolving if it is not going to die.

Negative theology does not deny the findings of positive theology but on the contrary makes them all its own. What it does do is to remember the infinite gap mentioned above as the felt experience of religious men, and realise that the concepts we have about God given to us by affirmative theology are quite simply infinitely inadequate to represent the living Reality. So much is this infinite gap vividly realised that the negative theologian finds himself saying that it is closer to reality and somehow more satisfying to *deny* all those human concepts like person, nature, divine field, good, etc. as they are applied to God rather than affirm them, because the Reality of God is so completely beyond human experience that it seems like nonsense to talk of God in those terms. Thus rather than say God is good or true, the divine field or a person, it is more true to say he is not-good, not-true, not a field, not a person. This latter way of saying things conveys more truth to the mystic than the positive way. Eventually he grasps that the best of all approaches to God is that of silence, because *no* human words, not even the negative ones, are adequate in the face of God, remembering the Chinese saying that 'he who knows Tao does not talk about it; he who talks about it does not know it.' It is important to see that this silence is not the silence of emptiness, but of richness. It is the deep silence of one who is speechless before the plenitude of God. The negative approach, in other words, has to grow out of the positive approach, otherwise it is merely empty; unknowing must be preceded by knowing, prayer by Bible reading and contemporary thought.

This brings us to the conclusion that knowledge of God must be an amalgam of positive and negative theology. The two approaches need each other. Nobody is entitled to choose only one form of knowledge; he must choose both, correcting the self-confidence of positive theology with the pessimism of negative theology. If there is too much 'unknowing' of God, our knowledge of him will get thinner and thinner as time goes on for lack of sustenance from the Bible, not to mention cross-fertilisation from the culture of the day, and spirituality will become a dusty abstraction out of touch with living thought. If there is too much 'knowing' of God, the vital element of agnosticism in Christianity will be forgotten and our knowledge of God will become anthropomorphic, with the result that we may forget that God is always bigger than any representation of him (even the representations given in the Bible) and begin to think that our definitions are the whole truth about him (a tendency many controversialists fall into). God is not a super-, blown-up version of man's thought but Mystery. That is why the Bible in the midst of all its anthropomorphisms about God maintains the tradition of the hidden, unimaginable God as well. There is a lesson for us all in Yeats's poem:-

THE INDIAN UPON GOD

I passed along the water's edge below the humid trees,
My spirit rocked in evening light, the rushes round my knees,
My spirit rocked in sleep and sighs; and saw the moorfowl pace
All dripping on a grassy slope, and saw them cease to chase
Each other round in circles, and heard the eldest speak:
Who holds the world between His bill and made us strong or weak
Is an undying moorfowl, and He lives beyond the sky.
The rains are from His dripping wing, the moonbeams from His eye.
I passed a little further on and heard a lotus talk:
Who made the world and ruleth it, He hangeth on a stalk,
For I am in His image made, and all this tinkling tide
Is but a sliding drop of rain between His petals wide.
A little way within the gloom a roebuck raised his eyes
Brimful of starlight, and he said: The Stamper of the Skies,
He is a gentle roebuck; for how else, I pray, could He
Conceive a thing so sad and soft, a gentle thing like me?
I passed a little further on and heard a peacock say:
Who made the grass and made the worms and made my feathers gay,
He is a monstrous peacock, and He waveth all the night
His languid tail above us, lit with myriad spots of light.

The lesson is that while we need models of God with which to live our religion in practice, we must always remember that those models, the new secular ones as much as the traditional biblical ones, are conditioned by our human situation, and that the first step in spiritual maturity is to 'sit loose to the image' (Bishop of Woolwich) and recognise the images we use as images and no more, so enabling ourselves to pass easily beyond them to the Absolute Reality which they represent and not become too preoccupied with controversy over their relevance. Preoccupation over terms in positive theology needs to be accompanied by a dose of negative theology. In this way a fruitful tension is built up between the two ways of knowing God.

At first impact this insight into the unknowability of God is a pessimistic one. The one ambition of the religious man – to know God – is unattainable in this life, and he seems to be doomed to produce a series of inadequate ideas as a substitute. But what at first sight seems frustrating is in fact the beginning of wisdom and the essential prerequisite for faith. For until we have grasped that no human idea ever comprehends God we have not broken out of our 'essentialism'; we are still living in a God-less world, content with idols of our own making, not the living God. The dissatisfaction and disillusion in the quest for God over the human tools of religion (dogma, liturgy, spirituality...) is the requisite preliminary kenosis for an authentic meeting with God. Just because God is above and beyond all human thought he is only genuinely encountered when 'religion', in the sense of man-made approaches to God, has been seen for what it is, a relative, provisional thing. At the heart of Christianity is a radical agnosticism – not about the existence of God but about what he is like. This agnosticism is the beginning of spirituality and is an essentially creative thing. In the pages that follow the reader must remember that human ideas and doctrines about God are only analogously true, not the absolute truth but sketchy limited shadows of the dazzling unlimited Reality which is God. Wisdom consists in recognising this at the beginning of the Christian response. We base our response on Christian doctrines but know that they do not fully comprehend the living truth. That is why the Christian response is always something more than the conceptual realisation of Christian doctrine, and is more satisfactorily comprehended by trying to live it than by merely reading and thinking about it. Often the simple Christian who lives his Christianity knows better than the theologian that all talk about God is limited and anthropomorphic. The fool is the man who forgets to be agnostic. He is sometimes a learned fool.

3. The Trinity and Man

So far in our discussion we have considered God exclusively as the One God and have not adverted to the central doctrine of Christianity, the Trinity. A spirituality which does not make the Trinity central is not Christian, for what distinguishes the Christian's approach to God from that of the non-Christian is his belief that in the hidden depths of the Godhead there are three Persons. (At this point we should remember what was established in the last chapter, that the use of human terms like 'person' of God is infinitely inadequate and almost misrepresentational. God is not three persons in the sense that three men are. It might be better to say he is personal in three ways.) Every time a Christian makes the sign of the cross he is making recognition of the Trinity, but few in fact ponder upon the significance of this central mystery. God is on the one hand solitary Being, distinct from creation, awe-inspiringly transcendent, the source and origin of all created being, the One Creator. But that is not the whole story. God is also in a mysterious manner Many. He is Father begetting the Son, Son the eternal image of the Father, Spirit the gift of love between the two, existing in an eternal dialogue of love since before the beginning of time. How this can be is a mystery, but it is part of revelation. Its ultimate significance is that in God men can find not only the meaning of unity in the world, but also the meaning of diversity. At the heart of the one God there is diversity, an everlasting dialogue between the Father, the Son and the Holy Spirit. This means that God is somehow open not shut, inviting not repelling, including not excluding, dialogue not silence, Love as well as Being. It gives the clue to the continual tension there is to be found in the world between the claims of unity and diversity, between the One and the Many. They both originate from God.

The mystery of the trinitarian Godhead gives the clue to the nature of man. All men find within themselves a conflict between two contradictory drives: the drive for separation and the drive for union. On the one hand man wants to be separate from other men, to be distinct, himself and not anybody else, working out his destiny for himself;

part of his personality development consists in being true to this instinct to be autonomous. On the other hand man finds in himself a desire not to be alone but to be united to other men, to enter into communication with his fellows, to be open, receptive, in partnership with the rest of humanity; so another part of his personality-development consists in making himself open to others, for persons fulfil themselves by relating to other persons, finding their autonomous selves in losing them in the various involvements of life. 'Through the Thou a man becomes I' (Buber). In other words there are drives in man in two opposite directions, and life for him means making that opposition fruitful and an agent of development, allowing the instinct for both being and love to be operative in his life. The ultimate reason for this is that, as announced in the New Testament, God himself is not only Being but also Love, and man is created in his image.

Man is not only created in the image of the Trinity, he is also recreated in that image. This latter phrase is not an empty one, but expresses a real truth, that redemption for man means a divinisation of his whole self, which St Paul did not hesitate to call being adopted into the family of the Blessed Trinity. According to him new life in Christ means being able to call God 'father' and Christ 'brother' and being a co-heir of the Son's redemption. It is not going too far to say that the Christ-life catches a man up into the Godhead while he still lives this earthly life. The perfectly correct philosophical notion of God as the ground of our being takes on a much more personal tone in the light of Christian revelation. It is the three Persons of the Trinity who are the ground of our being and source of life in this world. By baptism we are brought into the mysterious circle of the three divine Persons, and can call God father because Christ is our brother and the Spirit is within us enabling us to do so.

For all who are led by the Spirit of God are sons of God. For you did not receive the spirit of slavery to fall back into fear, but you received the spirit of sonship. When we cry 'Abba! Father!' it is the Spirit himself bearing witness with our spirit that we are children of God, and if children, then heirs, heirs of God and fellow heirs with Christ (Rom. 8.14–17).

We can truly say that the Trinity is the originating impulse of our life in this world.

The specific realisation of the trinitarian basis of our spiritual lives is a fairly recent rediscovery, for it is only in modern times that theologians have been willing to allow that the Christian has a distinct relationship to each Person of the Blessed Trinity. Formerly it was thought that to say this would derogate from the essential unity of the Godhead and seem to suggest that God's actions outside the Trinity were not one in essence. However theologians now concede that a Christian has distinct relations to each of the divine Persons, for it would be hard to explain the teaching of the New Testament in any other way. Christian spirituality, then, is an approach to the one God not from the outside but – and this is the astonishing truth – from the inside. Baptism raises us to the intimacy of being able to be a brother (by adoption) of Jesus Christ and a son (by adoption) of the Father and to share in the mutual gift of the Holy Spirit who is the Love of God. This is the approach of the liturgy too. It does not address God impersonally from afar, but prays to him as the Father through Jesus Christ the Son in the common unity of the Holy Spirit. It is not hard to see that this alters greatly the 'warmth' of our commerce with the incomprehensible God. It is not an impersonal worship of the unknown God, but a highly personal life within the circle of the Trinity. We are part of the Family – though the mystery remains and, if anything, becomes greater, a trinitarian God being even more incomprehensible than the One God of the philosophers.

We said in the first chapter that religion is the mutual presence of God to man and man to God. It can now be seen that the Christian religion involves a deeply mysterious and personal presence of the three Persons to man and *vice versa.* The presence of the three Persons to man is what is known as the indwelling of the Trinity, whereby to the soul of the baptised person the Father, Son and Holy Spirit are present in a special way. At the Last Supper Christ, having stressed his own unity with the Father – the Father is in him and he in the Father – then went on to stress how he would not leave his followers orphans but would remain with them in the person of the Holy Spirit the Comforter (Paraclete) who would be sent by the Father in his name. This means that all three Persons of the Trinity would be present to them. 'My Father will love him (the Christian) and we will come to him and make our home with him' (Jn 14.23). Nothing could be more explicit than these strong words: the Blessed Trinity is present by indwelling to the soul of the justified man. This gift of God himself to the baptised person is *uncreated grace.*

Furthermore the presence of God to man is creative and effects a real change in the soul of the Christian. God does not change, but in coming to man and dwelling within him he effects a change in him which a long tradition has dared to call man's divinisation. This is nothing less than the transformation of the man's whole self by his reception of the indwelling Trinity – his 'presence to God' in response to God's presence to him. Although based on man's nature and never contradicting it, it is nevertheless a raising up of man to a totally new, supernatural plane of living. God, then, is present to man by dwelling within him, and man is present to God, in return, by being raised to a supernatural level of existence which consists essentially in relating to the Father through the Son in the Holy Spirit. This change in man is *created grace.* We will have more to say about it later, for it is the theological basis of spirituality.

4. The Father speaks the Word

In the Bible there are many metaphors to describe the action of God in the world; he is the light which shines, food which nourishes, water which fertilises. But the phrase which is the most telling to describe the action of the Father towards mankind and which in fact underlies the whole concept of revelation is that of the Father speaking to men. The whole of the history of salvation is portrayed as a series of 'speakings' of God to men, from the first word by which the heavens were made (Ps 33.6-9), through the old covenant and sayings of the prophets which were considered as the word of God down to the New Covenant. Towards the end of the Old Testament the word of God was seen as increasingly personified, almost as a personal emissary of

God himself (cf. Is 55.10; Wis 18.44ff.). The final development of the idea came with the birth of Jesus whom the New Testament sees as, in person, the Word of God. The prologue to St John's Gospel and the opening verses of the Epistle to the Hebrews, both famous passages, introduce this idea and leave no doubt about the fact that Jesus is to be regarded as the Word of God in person, the culmination and surpassing of all the fragmentary words which God had spoken in former times.

In order fully to understand the teaching of the Bible on this it is as well to recall the meaning the term 'word' (*dabar*) had for the Hebrews. For them to speak and make use of words had a double significance only one of which we have in English. For them a word was not only an idea in the mind but the event, the deed which embodied that idea. Both the conceptual and actual content were taken into account. The shepherds at Bethlehem are described as saying, 'Let us go over and see this word which has come to pass.' Where we would be inclined to say, 'Let us go and see this birth and the meaning behind it,' they merely said, 'Let us see this word', a term which stood for both meaning and event. Hence for the Jews the idea that God spoke to men had a more existential significance than the mere handing on of information; it meant that God was speaking to men by acting upon them, and consequently each event in sacred history had a divine meaning behind it which men were intended to discern. And so all the divine actions to save men in the Bible, like the Exodus from Egypt or the Babylonian Exile, all the victories and defeats in war, the plagues and famines in peace, were seen as God's words to men. By these actions God was speaking to men. The long passage of events in the Old Testament is a history of the gradual unfolding to men of God's intentions for them, described by the prophets as God's word to men. The events were divine messages, the messages were events.

Then came the Incarnation and the New Testament, and God's word now takes on a further dimension of meaning. It is not only a *message* of salvation from God to men; nor is it only an *event* to save men set in motion by God. The further layer of meaning is now that God's word is a *Person*, Jesus Christ himself. This was the ultimate revelation of the

New Testament, that God's speaking to men had taken the form of sending his Son to be the perfect representation of himself and what he intended for men. ('Philip, he who has seen me has seen the Father' [Jn 14.9]). Where before God had been content to speak to men through divinely-guided events and divinely-inspired prophets, he now took the ultimate step of embodying his 'word' to men in the person of his Son, incarnated as the son of Mary. 'In many and various ways God spoke of old to our fathers by the prophets; but in these last days he has spoken to us by a Son.' (Heb 1.1-2). The Word of God since the New Testament has now three layers of meaning. It is a message of salvation, an event to save and the Person of Christ. The birth, life, death, Resurrection and Ascension of Jesus Christ were thus an immensely pregnant happening in terms of God's word to men.

The task of the Church is to keep alive the Word of God and transmit it faithfully to each generation, and Christian spirituality consists in the first place of listening to the Word of God, for, as we saw, Christianity is not man's initiative but his response to God. If we have understood what has been said about the Word of God, it will be seen that listening to the Word of God is something which has deeper implications than can be seen at first sight. The Word of God is message-event-Person, and therefore listening to the Word of God will mean not only receiving a message, but also participating in an event, and above all surrendering to a Person. These are three layers of that listening to the Word of God which is the first task in spirituality. Let us examine each briefly.

First there is listening to the Word of God considered as a message from God to us. This means primarily reading the Bible. It is the pillar and foundation of all spiritual living. It is true that we ought to read much else besides the Bible if we are to be intelligent Christians, but all theology is a commentary on the revelation of God in the Bible, and therefore the reading of Christians should be the Bible first and foremost. In reading the Bible the Christian allows himself to be guided by the Church, because of the Church's right and duty to interpret Scripture. There are two ways to read the Bible. One is to study it, more or less, according to our capacity for study. Here the findings of modern biblical scholarship are of great value and cannot afford to be neglected by any. This is essentially a masculine way of treating the sacred text, attacking it with zest for a greater understanding, subjecting it to scrutiny to find out what exactly the human author meant, and therefore by implication the Divine Author behind him. It is here especially that the guidance of the Church is needed. There is also a more feminine way of reading scripture, and this is the way of allowing the text to speak to the reader, remaining passive rather than active, slowly reading and pondering as one reads, allowing it to dissolve on the tongue like a lozenge, as Von Hügel described it. This is to remember that every word is the Word of God with a message not only for a time past in history but for the reader here and now. This latter way is the way that evangelical Christians have developed as the foundation of their spirituality by means of which they measure their lives daily against the Word of God. It is also the traditional '*lectio divina*' of the monks. It is essentially the sort of reading which requires patience and love, and is the only way to draw from the gospel its meaning for the individual. A fine example of it is given in W. E. Orchard's autobiography.

When he [Orchard's grandfather] came home from work, after his meal, he shaved, dressed himself more carefully, and then settled down to the Bible, set under the lamp on the table before him. When the Book had been opened at the proper place, his spectacles had to be carefully polished, to the accompaniment of anticipatory sighs over the treasures he was about to explore. The spectacles being then as carefully adjusted, a verse was slowly read, half aloud to himself. Deeper sighs then followed, perhaps accompanied by the exclamation 'This Blessed Book!' Further reflection would bring forth joyful tears, which meant that the spectacles had to be wiped again; and so on, but always with the same deliberation. A visiting minister used to tell how, coming in upon him one evening during these pious exercises, he inquired what was giving him such evident joy, and was told that it was the 8th of Romans: 'I have been on it all week,' he explained. 'And how far have you got?' 'The 5th verse,' was the reply; and this was Thursday night!

Secondly there is listening to the Word of God as a continuing event to save. This means listening to the Word of God in the liturgy and participating in it, for the liturgy is the present-day continuation of the redemption of men by Jesus Christ. We participate in the liturgy not only by listening to the public readings of the Bible which make up a good part of the Mass and sacraments, but also by joining in the ritual action which is the visible embodiment of Christ's action. Without stretching the imagination too far, this latter participation, as well as the actual listening to the readings, can be termed 'listening' to the Word, because the event-happening of the sacrament is itself the Word of God, and so joining in it with Christ is a form of 'listening' to him. If God speaks by events as well as words, then listening to the speech of God means participating in an event as well as listening to words. We will have more to say about the place of the liturgy in spirituality. At this point let us merely note that it is one of the basic forms of listening to the Word of God essential to Christian spirituality.

The third form of listening to the Word of God is the one which the other two lead to, viz. surrendering to the Person of Jesus Christ who is the Word of God. Here communication between the Father and mankind becomes most intimate and deep. The Father is speaking to men not only by messages through the prophets and apostles, not only by salvation-events like the sacraments, but most intimately through and in the person of his Son. The deepest form of communication back to God is by surrendering to the Person of the Word. The Son is the Father's Word to men, but at the same time, because he is the Head of the human race, the Son is our word back to the Father. Thus in the liturgy God speaks to us through Jesus Christ, and we dare to speak back to the Father through the same Jesus Christ. Divine-human communication, then, resolves itself into the beautiful simplicity of being conformed to the Person of Christ. By being as closely identified with him as possible the Christian is at one and the same time ensuring that his words to God are according to the mind of God and also that God's word for him is made manifest to him. Communication, in other words, between God and man since the Incarnation has become completely personal, for it is now not a question so much of an interchange of messages, but of an interchange of lives: the question of living more and more 'in Christ' and so of ensuring that we are in close contact with the Word of God. This communication by life rather than words is, of course, the goal of the deepest kinds of human intercourse – to get beyond a mere exchange of messages to something more profound and total, an exchange of lives, as in marriage. It is not surprising that God should have chosen it as the vehicle of his revelation to men.

5. *Jesus Christ our Brother*

(1) *The Christian Mystery*

Our consideration in the last chapter of the Hebrew use of the term 'word' helped us to see that for the Semitic mind an idea and the action that embodied it went together. Truth was not, as it tends to be for us, an abstract proposition, but an existential force, deed as well as concept. When, therefore, St Paul called the redemption of mankind by Christ a mystery (Ephesians and Colossians), he intended it to mean both a mysterious truth beyond the comprehension of man and also the event in which that mysterious truth took shape in history. Doubtless he was influenced by the use of the word in the contemporary mystery-religions which enjoyed a popularity in the Roman Empire, like Mithraism, but he used the word with considerable differences. It is more likely that he wanted to stress the ineffability of God's plan to save men in history and so called it a mystery, thus placing his positive thought about man's salvation firmly in the perspective of the negative theology we spoke about in Chapter 2. The important thing for us when we use the term is to remember that it denotes not only an abstract truth beyond our understanding but also the divine deeds in history by which that abstract truth came into operation in the world. Mystery means not only the plan in God's mind to save the world but also the events of that salvation in history. The events are as mysterious as the plan.

Our consideration in the last chapter will also have helped us to see that the mystery of salvation is an unfolding revelation. Jesus Christ did not appear among men without forerunners. There had been a preparation of the People of God through the Old Testament which reached its climax with the first coming of Christ and continues to 'grow' in the new People of God through these last days until the culminating event of the second coming of Christ. Because the mystery of salvation is incarnated in this world it is a *history*. We can, in fact, view the mystery of salvation in two ways: either in one glance as a unity, taking in the whole sweep of redemptive history and seeing it essentially as one – the eternal design of God to save all men in Christ; or we can view it step by step in all its various stages and growths beginning with the creation and ending with the second coming of Christ. Taken thus, the mystery has various points for examination: the ineffable plan in God's mind to save all men (cf. 1 Cor 1-4); the Old Testament 'growth' from the calling of Abraham to the preaching of John the Baptist, a long history of purifying preparation; the culmination of the mystery in the coming of the Word as a Person; the time of the Church when the mystery of Christ is present to us in the liturgical actions of the Church; the mystery in me, my sacramental union with the Risen Christ (these last three stages are referred to throughout Ephesians and Colossians – it is what those two epistles are about); finally the second coming of Christ and the completion of all in Him. In viewing the mystery thus strung out in successive stages it is important to refer each salvific episode to the one, eternal, never changing plan in the Father's mind to create and redeem all men. There is a deep unity in the diversity.

An important corollary to the fact that the mystery of salvation takes place across time, and that we in these days are situated between the first and second comings of Christ, is that we have two important time-relationships in our Christian lives. We look back and we look forward. In our lives there is an Already and a Not Yet. This gives rise to two distinct Christian actions, that of commemoration and that of eschatological hope. Christian spirituality and liturgy pivot between these two poles. Sometimes we are busy looking back, commemorating the events of salvation in the past which culminated in the death and resurrection of Christ; this is the mood of Christian thanksgiving and of Christian complacency – we are glad and thankful that redemption has already been effected and that the Presence of the Trinity accompanies us in our pilgrimage (by faith) through life. At other times we look forward and fill our minds with a striving forward to the goal not yet achieved, working out our salvation in fear and trembling. This is the mood of Christian hope, for in looking forward we do not put any trust in ourselves but only in the saving power of God. We are aware not only that we have many treasures already in our keeping, but also that we carry them in earthenware vessels. True spiritual balance consists in maintaining the tension between these two moods of Christian living, neither overdoing the looking back and so becoming dangerously complacent, nor overdoing the striving forward and so becoming pessimistic. Both moods can be found running through St Paul's epistles, for he is equally ready to tell his readers that they have already put on Christ or to tell them to put on Christ as if this had not yet been done. Both statements are true, for if we have already become new men in Christ, it has not yet appeared what we shall be when Christ comes again (1 Jn 3.2). We have grace already, but grace is meant to grow and is only the seed of glory. Finally let us note that both aspects of Christian living centre upon Jesus Christ. Looking back we see Christ in his first coming and give thanks (eucharist) for that; looking forward we see Christ in his second coming and centre upon him as our future hope. We are thus enveloped in Christ whichever way we turn: to the past, to the future, or to the present where Christ is in our hearts.

The Christian mystery is sometimes called the paschal mystery. Why? The adjective 'paschal' means 'pertaining to a passover or transition'. The Bible reveals the mystery of salvation always as happening in terms of a transition: from dark to light, from captivity to freedom, from desert to fertility, from barrenness to marriage, from death to life. God's acts to save men, from the calling of Abraham to leave his home to the climactic mystery of the passion, death and resurrection of Christ, always take the form of passover or exodus. This is no less true of the mystery of salvation in the Church and in our lives. Here too it is a question of passover or exodus from death to life. That is the pattern of Christian living in this world. It answers to a deep need in man to be 'saved from death'. Another way of saying this is to say that Christian spirituality is essentially sacrificial, for sacrifice is a passover from death to life, and what is paschal in character is sacrificial. In calling the Christian mystery the paschal mystery we call attention to the fact that Christian living is sacrificial because it is patterned on the redemptive act of Jesus Christ, who had to suffer before he entered into his glory (Lk 24.26).

(2) *The Body of Christ*

The purpose of the salvific will of the Father appears in the Bible as a communal one: to gather men together into a community who will be His People. We see this happening in the Old Testament under Moses and subsequent leaders of the Israelites, and in the New Testament the purpose of Jesus' life and death is also seen as 'to gather into one the children of God who are scattered abroad' (Jn 11.52). The history of the early Church is precisely the story of how the converts to Christ were gathered into the new People of God to live a life of intense fellowship, sharing their possessions and being held together by the liturgy (cf. Acts 2.44-47). Although this communal purpose of redemption was often soft-pedalled in later ages, the Church has never lost the conviction that

> It has pleased God, however, to make men holy and save them not merely as individuals without any mutual bonds, but by making them into a single people, a people which acknowledges him in truth and serves him in holiness (Vatican II, *Constitution on the Church* 9.)

Being baptised and introduced into the Christian mystery means for the individual membership of the Church.

The profoundest thought on this communal aspect of the Christian mystery was produced by St Paul with his teaching on the Body of Christ. As members of the Church Christians are members of the Body of Christ. This implies a twofold union. First, it means union of all members with each other – St Paul worked this out in 1 Cor 12.12-31 and Romans 12.4-8. Secondly, there is the deeper union of all

Christians with and in the Risen Christ – this is the teaching of Ephesians and Colossians. This latter union is the more profound and mysterious and is in fact the cause of the other. Because we are 'in Christ' we are united with one another. Being in the Church, then, involves us in a twofold union, the one to our fellow Christians, and beyond them to all men who are all members of a redeemed race and therefore at least inchoately in Christ; and the other to God as brothers and co-heirs of redemption with Christ.

Both these unions are made possible and effective by our union with Jesus Christ. He it is who makes it possible for us to love God and men, for it is in the power of his love that we relate in both directions. He not only gave us the two commands to love God and men but also through baptism and our union with him he gives us the power to carry them out. (Note that the union we have in Christ with our fellow Christians is not confined to those who are alive contemporaneously with ourselves; it stretches forward and backward in time. This means that the communion of the Body of Christ takes in the souls in purgatory and those who have gone before us to heaven, preeminent among the latter being our Lady, first of the redeemed. This is the theological basis for devotion to Mary and the Saints.)

We have said enough to show that Christian spirituality is primarily communal and corporate. This means two things:

a) The source and sign of spiritual progress is the liturgy, which is the worship by the Church, through its Head, of the Father. By participating in the liturgy Christians grow together in union with God. Because all advances to God are made through Christ, the one Mediator and Way, all personal advances in spirituality are linked in some way with the Mass and the sacraments. Liturgy does not preclude private, non-liturgical prayer; rather it encourages it. But private prayer is secondary to the liturgy.

b) The test of a Christian's invisible union with God is his visible union with his neighbour, and the two cannot be separated. This is the burden of Jesus' teaching on the Last Judgment (Mt 25.31-46) and of St John's First Epistle.

Confronted with the problem of unity man is ambivalent. On the one hand he feels within himself the urge to be united with all men, to go out of himself in love, but on the other hand there is in him a similarly strong urge to retire within himself and remain separate, a radical refusal to take root in the other. These are the two urges mentioned in Chapter 3 which reflect the unity and diversity of God. Today the urge to unity is strong. It is reflected in the thinking of secular humanism which sees hope for mankind in the technological, democratic and cultural revolutions taking place in the world, all of which point towards greater unity. It can also be seen reflected in Marxist thought, which over and above secular humanism has its powerful ideology of unity among men. Christians can find much in common with authentic movements among men for unity. The Christian, however, adds that the centre of unity among men is Christ, the first-born from the dead and Head of redeemed humanity, and maintains that outside the Body of Christ the movement for human unity is bound to be incomplete, for only the grace of Christ can overcome the deep-rooted divisiveness in man which tends to make him turn even his movements for unity into selfish pursuits. It is in fact the mission in the Church to bring all men together not merely in a political or cultural unity but in a union of heart and soul in the Risen Christ our Brother, so forming the true community of the brotherhood of men under the common Father. The liturgy is the chief instrument of this, for it is the prayer of Christ who 'is our peace, who has made us [both] one, and has broken down the dividing wall of hostility' (Eph 2.14).

(3) *Christocentric Spirituality*

Within the communal life of the Body of Christ the individual Christian has his own personal life in Christ. Very briefly, and necessarily inadequately, this can be summarised in three sentences:-

a) Christians are united to Christ.
b) They are united to Christ's redemptive act.
c) Their spirituality is christocentric.

a) St Paul uses frequently the phrase 'in Christ' to describe the union which Christians enjoy with Jesus Christ. By this phrase he is saying that the union which the baptised Christian has with Christ is more than merely one of *intentions*, being a truly ontological union. We are united with Christ by what we *are*. This union is achieved not by the ethical efforts of the Christian but by baptism. It is baptism which makes a man 'in Christ', not his personal efforts which build upon the initial gratuitous union. Thus Christian spirituality can be called a sacramental mysticism. The Christian is united with God by the sacraments, not by his own efforts. Under grace he uses his powers of effort to improve upon the initial union with God, but both the union itself and the growth are free gifts of grace.

b) If our Christian lives were only a union with Christ statically it would be remarkable enough. But the teaching of St Paul is that in some mysterious manner we are united to Christ dynamically – i.e. we are joined not only to him but also to his redemptive act. This is the unmistakable message of Romans 6.3-11:-

Do you not know that all of us who have been baptised into Christ Jesus were baptised into his death? We were buried therefore with him by baptism into death, so that as Christ was raised from the dead by the glory of the Father, we too might walk in newness of life. For if we have been united with him in a death like his, we shall certainly be united with him in a resurrection like his. We know that our old self was crucified with him so that the sinful body might be destroyed and we might no longer be enslaved to sin. For he who has died is free from sin. But if we have died with Christ, we believe that we shall also live with him. For we know that Christ being raised from the dead will never die again; death no longer has dominion over him. The death he died he died to sin, once for all, but the life he lives he lives to God. So you must consider yourselves dead to sin and alive to God in Christ Jesus.

We are joined not merely to Christ, but also to his paschal act, his death and his resurrection. Although we cannot fathom the full implications of this mystery, it may help if we break it down into two complementary statements which are contained in St Paul's words:- We are somehow part of Christ's passover; Christ is somehow part of our passover. *We are part of Christ's passover* – that is, we were not only redeemed *by* Christ but also *in* Christ. When Christ died and rose we died and rose in him. This is how St Paul prefers to present the truth of our being redeemed by Jesus. Our union with Christ transcends time. We were in him at his passover.

Christ is part of our passover – that is, our whole Christian life, our passage to heaven, is also Christ's. He dwells in us, is united to us here and now, identifies himself with our passage through life. 'It is no longer I who live but Christ who lives in me' (Gal 2.20), so that our daily life, in so far as it is a Christian one, is lived in Christ; our prayer, work, suffering, charity, eating, sleeping, everything, is not only ours, but it is Christ's in us. Our passover and Christ's have in a mysterious way joined up. The sacraments are the points in our life when this union with Christ is experienced most intimately, but they in turn influence the rest of our lives. The whole is lived in Christ to the Father. By baptism our entire secular lives are made sacred.

c) Christian spirituality is christocentric. If we have understood what has been said about our sacramental union with the Risen Christ, we will see that the primary sense in which our approach to God is centred on Christ is the sense of our being united to Christ to form a common *subject*. In and with Christ we approach the Father. The object of our prayer is the Father, while Christ is the subject praying with us and in us. (As we saw in Chapter 3, the Christ-life places us by adoption within the family of the Trinity; we call God our father and Christ our brother.) This is the way the liturgy chiefly regards Christ, not as an object of worship but as the mediator through whom we pray to the Father. It is only in a secondary sense that the Christian's prayer is christocentric with Christ as the *object* to whom he prays. This is a legitimate form of Christian prayer, as for instance in the mediaeval and post-tridentine devotions which have come down to us, like the Stations of the Cross, devotion to the Sacred Heart and the Precious Blood, Benediction of the Blessed Sacrament, but it is not the way the New Testament normally urges us to pray nor the primary way of the liturgy. Christ is the Way, not the Goal of life. We should not exaggerate the difference between the two approaches, for they are ultimately one, being based on the one Person of Christ. Nevertheless it ought to be understood that the way of making Christ subject rather than object of our devotions is the more biblical and authentic. It is also the one which allows more growth in spirituality, for it answers the two basic needs of man with regard to God: the need to see God as transcendent and other than self, and the need to see him as immanent and united to self. The first need is catered for by our relationship to the Father and the second by our relationship to the Son as our brother. We see the Father as Other, God who dwells in unapproachable light even though he is our father. We see Christ as our brother, so intimately united to us that we can say we are in Christ and he in us. Whereas making Jesus Christ, as opposed to the Father, the object ('out there') of spirituality can easily degenerate into a merely human admiration of Christ as hero and does not allow for the basic mystical needs of man described in Chapter 2.

6. The Holy Spirit and the Life of Grace

We saw in Chapter 3 that the presence of God to men since the Incarnation and Redemption is none other than the indwelling of the Blessed Trinity. Going further we have seen that this indwelling of God is an active presence, the Father speaking the Word to us, the Son our brother making reply on our behalf, for we are inserted into his paschal mystery. This presence of God to us is called uncreated grace. As we have seen, uncreated grace has a creative effect on man which transforms and elevates his life and has been called his divinisation. This is created grace. As St Augustine said, '*Quia amasti me, fecisti me amabilem.* Because you have loved me [uncreated grace], you have made me lovable [created grace].' In the Bible the agent of this transformation is the Holy Spirit. He is the Spirit who spoke through the Old Testament prophets, who overshadowed the Virgin Mary at the Incarnation when Jesus was conceived, and who came down upon Jesus at his baptism at the start of his public life. Now he is the agent of sanctification in the Body of Christ, the living link between regenerated man and God, transforming him into a son and enabling him to cry, 'Abba! Father!'.

The important thing is to see created grace in terms of the indwelling of God – it is man's reaction to God's presence – and not to think of it as some sort of spiritual 'stuff' poured into our souls to change them and existing quite apart from the presence of God. It is true that grace transforms us into new persons, but the change is one of personal relationship with the indwelling God and not a quality added on to man in isolation from God. Still less is grace a quantitative thing, and if we speak of increases and decreases in grace it has to be understood that we are speaking of a growing or diminishing relationship to God, not of more or less supernatural energy. Grace is not stuff but 'a permanent disposition which capacitates man for an I-Thou relationship with God, and is manifested in the personal communication of faith, hope and charity.' (Fr Juan Alfaro). In other words the Holy Spirit makes us love God with a 'divine' love. This 'divine' love is grace. It is our inspired reaction to God's love for us.

What is this inspired reaction to God? It is a relationship of knowing and loving God. 'This is eternal life, that they know thee, the only true God, and Jesus Christ whom thou hast sent' (Jn 17.3), says St John. In our more analytical way we can describe it as love of God based on knowledge of him. In heaven there is the vision of God face to face, but here our knowledge of him is in the hidden way of faith. So our Christian, graced, response to God in this life is charity based on hope and faith. The I-Thou relationship between us and God is made up of faith, hope and charity. These are called the theological virtues because they relate us directly to God. They form the encounter between the soul and God. Basically they are an act of prayer – believing in him, hoping in him, loving him. Prayer is the chief action of the life of grace, the sacramental mysticism, spoken of in the last chapter, in operation.

Our relationship to God is not only made up of the direct contact of prayer. It also consists of the acts of our life, our works, which we do for God, in Christ, under grace. Together with the theological virtues the graced soul also possesses supernatural moral virtues, its acquired virtues 'graced'. These are the acquired habits of acting ethically (e.g. patience, kindness, truthfulness, purity...) which the good life manifests. They are part of the Christian response to God and so are supernatural virtues. It is a matter of secondary importance how these moral virtues are listed; they can for instance be listed loosely and not particularly scientifically, as in St Paul's Epistles, or they can be summed up under the four headings of the Greek philosophers: Prudence, Justice, Fortitude and Temperance, and then subdivided, as they were by scholastic theologians. The important thing is to see that they go along with the theological virtues and are inseparable from them. The view that prayer and works are unconnected, that faith-hope-charity and the moral virtues are quite separate, is quietistic and alien to the Christian message. My faith inspires my charitable acts towards my neighbour as much as it does my prayer. Even in the Old Testament the prophets inveighed against those who thought that ritual worship with no thought for social justice was sufficient to please God: and it was one of the main points of Jesus' teaching against those who only kept the letter of the Law, that the test of closeness to God was in works of charity not merely in prayer. In other words the only true I-Thou relationship to God is one which springs from an integrated life and is a response of the whole person to God; not merely one of the lips, but one which represents the whole life of the speaker.

The Christ-life of faith, hope and charity develops under the inspiration of the Holy Spirit. Over and above this ordinary development, the Holy Spirit sends his charisms upon individuals in the Church for the good of the whole. Whether these gifts are miraculous pentecostal happenings given for the Church or merely ordinary gifts and insights also for the Church, it is important that the whole Body be aware of the presence of the Holy Spirit thus acting in its midst, and so be ready to discern these gifts and act accordingly. The post-Tridentine Church has tended to think of these gifts as being given only to those in authority in the Church, but this is not the case. Anyone in the Church is liable to receive the 'burden' of a charism and it should not be thought that inspired initiative comes only from above in the Church. It is a feature of ecclesial life today that this is being increasingly realised both in theory and fact. Charisms, however, are over and above the covenant of grace and are given for the Church not for the individual. The baptismal infusion of faith, hope and charity remains the essential Christian gift and responsibility, and the way to heaven.

Grace is the seed of glory. There is an intrinsic connection between the life of grace here and the life of the vision of God in heaven. The former is the seed of the latter, the latter the fruition of the former. This is a way of saying that eternal life, the Christ-life, begins at baptism not at death. In this life we are already joined to God in grace, and at death will pass into a more direct union, which is vision. The whole meaning of grace is that eternal life has already begun in us. This is the message of St Paul with his insistence on our union with Christ now, and St John with the 'realised eschatology' of his gospel. There is, of course, much difference between the union of grace, which is hidden and sacramental (by faith), and tenuous and liable to be lost (by hope), and the union of glory when we will no longer see 'in a mirror dimly' but face to face for ever. It is fruitful here to bear in mind the tension mentioned in Chapter 5 between the Already and the Not Yet. Already we are in Christ by grace, but not yet with him in glory. The spiritual life is the passover from one to the other under the inspiration of the Holy Spirit.

PART II

Elements of the Christian Response

In the first part of this book we saw how the dogmatic facts of the Christian faith determined the pattern of the Christian life, for the latter is the response to the former. We saw that this response, which is man's commerce with God, takes the form of personal relationships to each of the three Persons of the Holy Trinity, listening to the Father's Word, participating in the Body of the Risen Christ, being pliant to the movements of the Holy Spirit within us, i.e. to grace. In the next chapters we examine from man's point of view what in terms of human commitment is involved in the carrying out of these three relationships, i.e. what man must do to be a faithful son of God in his present situation. These commitments are the elements of 'Christian spirituality'. In doing so, let us not forget that what we are doing is to analyse into separate elements something which in real life is not lived in distinct compartments, but like all human relationships is a living whole.

7. To Put on Christ

Can the Christian response be expressed in a short sentence? St Paul called it 'to put on the Lord Jesus' (Rom 13.14), and claimed that he was in travail for his converts till 'Christ was formed in them' (Gal 4.19). That in a nutshell is what our response must be as members of the Body whose Head is Christ. By 'putting on Christ' or allowing him to be formed in us we ensure that our life in this world is intimately united to the Son, in being and behaviour, and consequently that we are pleasing to the Father, whose design it is that we should come to him through the Son but get nowhere and do nothing salutary apart from him. Putting on Christ is a blanket phrase which is hard to understand for anyone who is not trying to do it, but which makes more sense to one who is. This is as it should be, because Christianity is a Way (Acts 9.2) and can therefore only be understood by living it and not by examination in the abstract. Having the 'mind of Christ' is not a question of book-learning but of living. So if a book like this has any use it is as a commentary on the Christian response during and after the event, not as a blueprint before it. It is not really possible to conceptualise the putting on of Christ because it is an experience of a living Person, and what follows is therefore put forward with the understanding that these are but dry bones of a living reality which is beyond explanation. As far as possible we will stick to the categories given by Jesus himself to describe his Way, and not provide our own.

Having the mind of Christ means imitating him. This means two things: being steeped in the knowledge of the Person Jesus who lived two thousand years ago, and also, for he is alive now, risen and glorified, participating in him as a living Reality whom we encounter in all the secular realities of this world but especially in the sacraments, by means of which our lives become his life in the union of grace. In other words we grow into the mind of Christ by knowing about him (studying the gospels) and by knowing him (the Christian life accompanied by prayer). The more we do this the more we will be assimilated to the Person of Jesus Christ and so 'put him on'.

In Jesus we see a man who made a complete surrender to the Father. He regarded himself as the one sent by the Father, whose 'meat' was to do what the Father wanted; he did not act except to carry out the designs of the Father, and the Father was well pleased with him. We see this complete oneness with the Father simultaneously fed and symbolised by the nights Jesus spent praying to the Father. Busy as he was, he yet went apart and prayed all night to God. Jesus also surrendered himself to the needs of his neighbour. His public life was lived at the beck and call of men, being their servant, available day and night to men's needs. The foxes had holes but the Son of Man nowhere to lay his head. This surrender to men is described in parables like the Good Samaritan and the Good Shepherd and exemplified in practice by all Christ's actions in the gospel – it is not possible to select a particular one to demonstrate this universal availability, for they all do. This complete sharing in the life of men by One who was the Son of God set in motion the process which is today called the secularisation of religion. Jesus shared to the full the life of men and kept apart from nothing which was human, to the extent of shocking the strict Jews by eating and drinking with sinners and talking with Samaritan women. For him, evidently, the whole of human life was sacred and 'religious', not just special parts of it like prayer and fasting. The Movement he started did away with the sacred separations associated up to then with religion. Christian love meant all men being one in Christ, with no distinction between Jews and gentiles, men and women, masters and slaves, priests and laity, saints and sinners. Secularisation is thus the working out in practice of the conditionless love of God and men enjoined by Jesus.

This twofold surrender – to God and man – reached its point of supreme fruition in the passion and death of Jesus. This was the Good Shepherd laying down his life for his sheep, the obedient Son undergoing death to fulfil the Father's design. Never was Jesus more 'surrendered' in both directions than at that point on Calvary when he delivered up his life into his Father's hands for his brethren. The whole of Jesus' life, in fact, can be explained by this twofold surrender, for instance his attitude to the Law and the externals of religion, which he regarded as relative to love and not absolute, and his attitude to sinners with whom he supped and whom he gathered round him as friends and followers. He manifested these attitudes because for him what mattered were the demands of people, his Father and his brethren, and not in the first place traditions and laws. Finally, it was his own prescription for perfection: first to love God with all heart, soul, mind and strength, and secondly to love neighbour as oneself. 'There is no other commandment greater than these,' he said (Mk 12.31). Having the mind of Christ means fully accepting this statement and living it, as he did. It covers the whole of Christian perfection.

In the New Testament St John and St Paul repeat this teaching. St John's First Epistle is an elaboration of the command of Jesus to love God and men. St John insists on both loves, and shows the inner connection between the two: each is a manifestation of the other; they are but separate aspects of the same thing.

In St Paul's Epistles also there is this simplicity of approach. St Paul dealt with complex issues in his letters and more than any other New Testament writer examined the theological depths of the Christian message, but in his passages on Christian living there emerges always a simple idea: that men's conduct should follow from, not precede, the Christ-life; in other words, Christian conduct must be the overflow of union with God, not the approach to it. In his epistles the moral exhortations are there but they come at the end of the letters after he has expounded the theological message; the lists of virtues to be embraced and vices to be avoided follow the expositions of the Christ-life and appear not so much as things to be done as things that will in fact be done by the man who is in Christ. In other words St Paul sees the essence of Christian living not in conduct to be observed, but in *being in Christ,* an inner state of love from which good actions flow. It is the sacramental union of being causing that of behaviour (cf. Chapter 5).

In chapter 13 of the First Epistle to the Corinthians St Paul explicitly expounds his views on the Christian life. This chapter is worth reading closely because St Paul is dealing with the problem facing us here: what exactly does putting on the Lord Jesus consist in? What is the Way for Christ's followers? It is not, as the Corinthians were inclined to think, the possession of extraordinary gifts and charisms, 'tongues of men and angels' or 'prophetic powers', however desirable they be (verses 1-2). Nor is it heroic deeds by themselves, like giving away all that one has or dying for the faith (verse 3). It is not knowledge, because knowledge of God in this life is imperfect as in a mirror dimly (verses 8-12). It is charity, which contains all the virtues and is the spirit behind heroic deeds and charisms making them worthwhile in the sight of God (verses 4-7). St Paul does not exclude deeds and charisms but points out that the Christian exercises them out of love, and if not, then they are useless. This is merely saying in another way that Christian conduct follows on from the Christ-life and is not worth anything by itself. Love is, in fact, the inspiration of all the virtues, the one that 'binds everything together in perfect harmony' (Col 3.14).

From this chapter in First Corinthians we are in a position to say briefly what putting on Christ is not and what it is. It is not one of three things which are often mistakenly taken as the essence of good Christian living. In the first place it is not external actions or great deeds. In all ages of Christianity there has been this tendency to externalise the Christian message and make it consist essentially in actions. The Pharisees did this when they made observance of the Law the essence of good living; there have been people willing to turn Christianity into observance of law in all ages since Christ. It is understandable because external deeds are observable by men and it is always a temptation to want to measure one's Christianity by observation and so achieve security. But this is to try and gain security outside Christ and to turn one's back on living by faith. Putting on Christ is not an affair of external actions but of love. Another form of this externalisation of religion is to be seen in those who think Christian perfection consists in doing great, austere deeds; we revere the man who fasts or wears a hairshirt as 'a saint'. Once again this is to turn the following of Christ away from love to non-essentials, like 'giving away all I have' or 'delivering my body to be burnt'.

Secondly, Christian perfection does not consist in the possession of supernatural powers. This is adequately dealt with by St Paul in the passage mentioned above. There has frequently been the tendency for Christians to be disproportionately overawed by miracles and to make the charismatic who is the recipient of such graces a model of the Christian life. This is to reject love in favour of moving mountains and speaking with tongues of angels. Pentecostal phenomena are indeed gifts from God but they are not the ordinary development of grace for all Christians. This latter is the gift of faith, hope and charity.

Lastly, the Christian life is not a special knowledge possessed by an inner few of selected persons, the Elect. Here is a third counterfeit which has appeared from time to time in the history of the Church – the rejection of the gospel in favour of a gnosis for the few. The Albigensians in the Middle Ages and the Quietists in seventeenth century France, for instance, manifested this aberration. In modern times it sometimes takes the form of an obsessive devotion to the higher ways of prayer, or depth psychology, or the new theology, pursuits which of their nature are for only a few chosen persons and not for the masses. Whatever form this imbalance takes, it is a misrepresentation of the Christian life because it places the following of Christ chiefly in the region of knowledge rather than in the region of love and life.

Christ's command however is clear and simple. The way to the Father is to follow the Son, and following the Son means observing his twofold, all-embracing commandment of love. 'And I will show you a still more excellent way' (1 Cor 12.31).

8. The Love of God

The first call of the Christian life is to love God above all things. This is what Jesus did. So being formed in Christ for us will result firstly in this. The grace of the Holy Spirit within us sanctifies our natural love for God by uniting it to the love the Son has for the Father. This is our supernatural love of God. 'Through Christ we have access in one Spirit to the Father' (Eph 2.18). This means that the Christian life is a life of love, a being 'decentralised', going out to, becoming concerned for, taking root in the Other who is God. This is not only done in specific periods of life which we call 'prayer', but must be the movement of the whole life of a man, the development of his whole self. In theory it can be considered separately under its aspect of a natural development, for man is also made naturally for union with God; but in the actual situation man finds himself in, which is the order of redemption, it is a supernatural development which takes place because man is baptised into union with the Holy Trinity and takes his place alongside the Risen Christ as an adopted son who says, 'Abba! Father!' Saying 'Abba Father' is loving God above all things, recognising him as the source and origin of all life.

In love there can be distinguished two elements, viz., the love that takes and the love that gives. They are not so much two loves as two aspects of one love. On the one hand man loves and wishes to use, to draw towards himself, to possess, to direct, even to command. On the other hand man loves and surrenders himself, goes out towards, wishes only what is good for the beloved, submits, obeys. The first movement is the love that takes, the second the love that gives. They are not, as we have said, two loves, but two aspects of one love; as it were the breathing in and the breathing out of the soul of man. There is no love which does not contain both elements.

The love man has for God therefore develops in both ways. Under the inspiration of the virtue of charity man develops his giving love, progressively going further beyond himself to God till he makes his life a complete surrender to the will of the Father and realises his sonship, in Christ, to the full. Under the inspiration of the virtue of hope man develops his taking love. It is wrong to think that this 'selfish' love disappears as grace develops in a man. It does not disappear but is progressively purified, man being led to hope less for God's gifts (finite securities, religious consolations, successes..., and more for God's gift of himself. The desire for God remains and is never superseded, but it centres finally on God himself, not on his gifts (See Chapter 15). This is the virtue of hope, which Jesus appealed to in his preaching as much as to the virtue of love, making no bones about promising us a treasure in heaven as the reward of our commitment to him. Christian *hope* teaches us that this treasure in heaven is none other than union with God himself, the object of Christian *love*. Under hope and charity the two aspects of love converge upon the Reality of God. We desire at the same time to possess God for ourselves and to surrender to him – like all lovers.

Both hope and charity are based on faith in this life. It is the foundation of the Christian approach to God, the basis of the commitment whose two aspects are hope and charity, the love that takes and the love that gives. Faith is as personal as hope and charity. We do not have faith in abstractions like 'revelation' but in God revealing truths to us through the Person of his Word. It is true that our faith commits us to credal statements formulated by the Church. Without them faith would be discarnate and nebulous. But we only believe in the credal statements because we first of all have committed ourselves in faith to the Son of God. It is our personal faith in him that makes us believe things about him.

Man's approach to God is therefore eminently personal, an amalgam of the three personal virtues of faith, hope and charity. These three are closely intertwined and only in theory separable. Believing in God leads inevitably to hoping in him, for what our belief tells us about a merciful and loving God rouses our hope. And hope leads inevitably to charity, for hoping in the gift of God himself to us prompts us to surrender ourselves completely to him (cf. Rom 5.1-5). In other words faith, hope and charity are three aspects of the one commitment a Christian makes to God under the inspiration of the Holy Spirit – the 'yes' he says to God from baptism onwards. This commitment is supremely personal – each individual's personal response (in the Church) to the personal, triune God. To talk of God in impersonal terms like Supreme Reality, Ultimate Meaning, Ground of our Being, without also recognising that he is Father, Son and Holy Spirit demanding our personal devotion, is to pick and choose from the New Testament revelation. As we saw in Chapter 1 we need both kinds of concept for our understanding of the God who has revealed himself to us. The impersonal, philosophic concepts prevent us from becoming too anthropomorphic about God, and the biblical, personal ones from being too donnish and sophisticated. True balance comes from remembering, as we did in Chapter 2, that *all* images of God, secular as well as theistic, have eventually to be discarded in the journey to God which is our pilgrimage in this life. 'The spiritual man . . . must remember that not only bad things, but even those that are good, may become hindrances if they are loved or sought inordinately, just as plates of gold held before the eyes prevent sight as effectively as plates of iron' (Louis de Blois). All the mystics bear witness that man is naked of all images in the true encounter with God. Meanwhile, if we are still progressing towards that imageless consummation and have not yet reached it (as most honest readers will admit), we may find both models for the approach to God helpful, sometimes coming before God as Father, 'out there', whom we adore and love, at other times surrendering to the Divine Force which rises within us like sap in the tree trunk, and enables us to perform all we do as actions in Christ, and so to 'pray our life'.

An invariable concomitant to loving God on the part of man is a sense of his own sinfulness. Contact with God if it is genuine produces in man the sinner a sense of sin which threatens at times to be overwhelming. This is right and proper, and is one of the tests of the genuineness of the approach to God, for contact with God is contact with Reality, and man therefore is faced with the reality of his sinfulness as soon as he adverts to the presence of God. It is not going too far to say that a Christian life which fails to produce this sense of sin is not based on truth but on falsehood. We are not here saying that a sense of human failure produces Christianity, but that Christianity highlights a sense of failure and inadequacy in man. We agree with Bonhoeffer that religion should not be forced upon man in his weakness, on the borders of life, but in his strength, at the centre. It is, however, precisely in finding Christ at the centre of life, in his strength as well as his weakness, that man realises with blinding clarity how inadequate he is. The strength of man as much as his weakness points to the need for God.

Part of Christian love is therefore penitence for sin. Asking pardon is part of loving God. As we shall see in Part III, this sense of sin does not diminish but grows with closeness to God and is quite compatible with Christian optimism, as long as it is based on the truth and not on morbid fantasies. When it is based on truth it is the ground for true Christian hope (and therefore love). We cannot hope in God genuinely unless we know the reality about ourselves and face up to it honestly, which is that we are sinners in need of forgiveness. In all ages holy men and women have shown this sense of sin as part of their love of God. It has little to do with temperament; optimistic persons like Pope John have been as much aware of their sinfulness and failures (cf. his Journal) as natural pessimists like the Curé d'Ars. St John in his epistle puts it this way:-

If we say we have fellowship with God while we walk in darkness, we lie and do not live according to the truth; but if we walk in the light, as he is in the light, we have fellowship with one another, and the blood of Jesus his Son cleanses us from all sin. If we say we have no sin, we deceive ourselves, and the truth is not in us. If we confess our sins, he is faithful and just, and will forgive our sins and cleanse us from all unrighteousness. If we say we have not sinned, we make him a liar, and his word is not in us (1 Jn 1.6-10).

There is a close connection between loving God and adoring him. Adoration flows out of the love that gives. An essential ingredient of love is the element of admiration and submission to the beloved. When the beloved is sovereign Lord and infinite God, then this admiration becomes absolute praise and the submission absolute adoration. There is therefore no contradiction between loving God and adoring him. They are but two aspects of the worshipful response to the Reality of God.

We said that the Christian response to loving God above all things and with our whole heart is not something which is done only at specific times of prayer in a man's life and then forgotten for the rest of living. This is the error of trying to find God in the 'gaps of life' and not in life itself. We saw in Chapter 5 that everything a Christian does in Christ is an act of love of God, not only his 'religious acts'. True lovers of God will, however, want to have periods of pure prayer as well as activity, in which to show God they love him. These periods of prayer are not escapes from loving God in life, but essential parts of that life of love. By grace man is admitted to a familiarity with God which is quite beyond his dreams; it is a state of being an adopted member of the family of the Trinity. Another biblical image says that the Christian is espoused to Christ. If we are to take these images seriously it means that we have to recognise that the comprehensive Christian life will contain not only periods of activity but also periods of repose, and that both of these can be means of being united to God. Furthermore, what might be called the marital balance of our lives in Christ will depend on a right proportion between these two. The wife who spends all her time sitting conversing with her husband instead of looking after the needs of the household, and the wife who neglects to speak to her husband because she is too busy, are both at fault because they have offended against this proportion. This is frankly metaphor, but the biblical revelation prompts us to apply it to the life of the love of God. We must not only work for God every moment of life; be must also make some of those working moments of life periods of conversing with God and telling him we love him, i.e. praying. Even if we did not have the example of Jesus in this matter we should still know that the covenant of grace demands prayer as the supreme way of loving God, first the prayer of the assembled Church in the liturgy, secondly the prayer of the individual child of God. It is true that as a Christian matures his life unifies within him and the distinction between loving God in activity and loving him in prayer becomes increasingly superficial. But the distinction never entirely disappears in this life and it is always true that our love of God must be exercised both in prayer and in activity. The point is that both are necessary and feed each other, otherwise there is an imbalance.

9. The Love of Men

The second call of the Christian is to love his neighbour as himself. The Christian task of loving God brings with it the task of loving everyone, because they are sons and daughters of God and inextricably bound up with him. The Christian life is therefore a being 'decentralised', going out towards, becoming concerned for, taking root in not only the Other who is God but also the other who is our neighbour. There is no question of the Christian being a man who goes out to God but otherwise keeps himself to himself, as if he could love God without also loving the children of God, and as if God were not part of this world and in every man. Jesus Christ asks that his followers lose themselves completely in the love of their neighbour precisely because loving God demands loving men as well. It is the basic both-and of the Christian religion. The pages of the gospel show Jesus by example and precept teaching his followers this truth that involvement in God means involvement in men. The Christ-life therefore involves for the individual not only an approach to the Father in Christ but also an approach to our brothers in Christ. It is one single movement.

Christ continues the work of reconciliation begun by himself in the world through his followers in the Church until his second coming. It is the work of spreading love in the world. He dwells with his brethren constantly and enables them to love each other, so that it is the mark of Christians that where they are to be found, there charity and fellowship is too. Lacordaire described a Christian as 'a man to whom Jesus Christ has entrusted other men.' Christ is both the sign that love is among men and also he in whom men love. 'Always, when I act as charity bids, I have this feeling that it is Jesus who is acting in me; the closer my union with him, the greater my love for the sisters without distinction,' was the experience of St Thérèse of Lisieux. The members of the Body of Christ know that the power to love other people is given them through their union with the Risen Christ, like their power to love the Father. These are the duties and gifts given them at baptism.

As with loving God so with loving men there can be distinguished two elements in loving, the love that takes and the love that gives. The first is the urge man has to take pleasure in other people, the second is the urge he has to give pleasure to others and work for their good. There is little that needs to be said about this second love, that consists in giving, since all men recognise it as the highest form of loving, and though it is difficult to practise it is the easiest to understand. True friendship and love drive a person to undertake all things in order to please and help another – even to the point of sacrifice, the extreme test of love. The man who is prepared to go out of his way to help another person and suffer for him shows the truest love. This is the point of Jesus' parables like the Good Samaritan and especially of his own passion and death for men. Here love for others went as far as it could to break down the barriers between self and others, uprooting the deep-seated refusal to take root in the not-I, which is in all men. By losing his life in other men, Jesus found it. Furthermore Jesus expected his followers to love their brethren with the same generosity as he had shown.

This is my commandment, that you love one another as I have loved you. Greater love has no man than this, that a man lay down his life for his friends (Jn 15.12-13).

Hearing this, the Christian who follows his Master is bound to be afraid. But he can silence his fears, for he will find complete personal fulfilment in the very moment he appears to be losing everything most precious to him. Jesus himself showed that the way for a man to find his life is to lose it in his love for others. Life in the Body of Christ, symbolised and fed by the Eucharist, is meant to lead people further and further into this fulfilment of love by losing self. It is, together with the worship of the Father, what the Church is all about. The work of redemption carried on by the Church is the work of reconciling not only men to God in Christ, but also men to each other in Christ. 'That is the meaning of the Cross (of redemption): at once the height and depth of contemplation and the length and breath of charity' (Daniélou).

We are meant also to *take* pleasure in loving other people, i.e. to exercise our desires for union with other men and women. Jesus' delight was to be with the sons of men. He gave people pleasure and took pleasure from them equally. The gospel does not discourage our natural attractions to other people; as always, grace builds on and does not destroy nature. However the fact that it is finite men and women that we desire places certain conditions on our love. When we desire God the desire is an absolute one, because God is absolute. He is the supreme good for us and there is no need to place any restrictions on our desire for him. It can and should be without limit. With our desire for men, however, it is different. Our love for them cannot be an absolute one but must be conditional – the conditions being there because of the creaturehood of man. No other man is our absolute good; he is always relative good for us, that relativity being determined by the fact that he and we are creatures under the one God Creator. The first condition of our love of men is that we give God his due. This means making our love for the other dependent on God's demands – in other words our demands must take lower place and fit in with God's. The second condition is that we give the other person his due. This means that we do not try to possess him for ourselves – in other words our demands must take lower place and fit in with those of the person himself. That first condition of giving God his due means that we must not let our love for another lead us both into offending God or in any way lessening our service of him. We must promote, not diminish, our mutual love of God. The second condition of giving the person himself his due means that we must not try to take over or possess another person as if he belonged to us. We must promote, not diminish, his personal development. The first is the condition of keeping the law of God. The second is the condition of poverty of spirit, of loving other people for themselves and not for self.

Another way of stating the difference between the love we must have for God and the love we must have for men is to say that our love for God must be absolute attachment, but our love for men must be a conditional attachment. The latter rather academic phrase states the teaching of the gospel on loving men. It is first of all an attachment. Our love for all the things of this world must be a sincere and warm attachment. People and things are not 'occasions' for showing our love for God by having the right intentions towards men. The sort of thinking which made loving men a matter of having right intentions and passed over or denied the fact that men were lovable in themselves is rightly seen nowadays as a misinterpretation of the message of Jesus. He taught that the world is lovable in itself and must be loved for its intrinsic goodness. It is a travesty of Christian teaching to say that the world of people and things is evil. It is therefore a mistake to think that lack of love for this world is a desirable thing. It is, on the contrary, a weakness which Christianity ought to correct.

If one would raise oneself to the eternal, it is not enough to depreciate the temporal. To raise oneself to grace, it is not enough to depreciate nature. To raise oneself to God, it is not enough to depreciate the world. ...People believe that, because they have not the strength (and the grace) to belong to nature, they belong to grace. They believe that because they lack temporal courage, they have passed the threshold of the eternal. They believe that because they have not the boldness to be worldly, they are godly; not brave enough to be on man's side, they believe that they are on God's side; not belonging to man, they think they belong to God. Because they love nobody, they believe they love God. And yet Jesus Christ was a man (Péguy).

Nevertheless the attachment we Christians have for this world should be a non-possessive one. The very creaturehood of what we love postulates a recognition of it in our love, as explained above. In other words true love of people and things requires in us a poverty of spirit to prevent our love of them being merely selfish and swamping them and us. By exercising the spirit of the beatitudes towards the good and lovely things of this world we will be liberated from a tendency to love them selfishly. Thus liberated, our love for people and things will enable us to see the true goodness in them without the distortions of selfish love, and the result will be not only a liberation for ourselves in the vision of beauty but also the persons loved will be freed from being bound to us by the bonds of our possessiveness. St Francis of Assisi was an example of a man whose love for this world was immensely strengthened and increased by his rigorous poverty of spirit. His detachment made him appreciative of the goodness of this world and attached him to it in a pure way. Detachment, in this context, is another word for true love. So far from being a holding back from life in this world, it is the supreme condition of involvement in it. The man who has not faced the problem of poverty of spirit in his love for the world has not yet begun to grow in that love. Once we begin seriously to love it is inevitable that we undergo this 'passivity of growth' which love brings with it.

Christian love for this world steers a middle course between hedonistic and puritanical tendencies. Both extremes are unchristian since they deny the meaning of the Incarnation and Death of Jesus. Hedonism is wrong because it leads a man to make himself an absolute in his love and so forget his own creaturehood and that of those he loves. Puritanism is wrong because it denies the goodness of God's creation and projects the tendency towards evil that is in us all on to objects outside ourselves. It is not beauty or possessions, sex or money, which is evil but the tendency in us to misuse these things. It is, in fact, equally a mistake to deny either the goodness of things in the world or the existence within us of an evil tendency to misuse this goodness. The Christian fight is against the tendency in us which is from original sin and bad, not against the world outside which is from God and good. It is important to distinguish the real enemy. Jesus demands that our unregenerate and wrongful love for people and things of this world be replaced; but we must be careful to replace the wrong sort of love of the world with the right sort of love, not with hatred. The right sort of love is a purified, liberated love, the love that springs from poverty of spirit. If this is understood it will be seen that certain consecrated Christian phrases like 'renouncing the world' and 'hating the flesh' have to be carefully interpreted according to their strict biblical meaning if they are not going to be misused and cause harm, as also does a book like *The Imitation of Christ* with its pessimism about the world.

We must recognise that this distinction also applies to love of self as well as love of others. The wrong sort of self-love needs replacing with the right sort of self-love, not with self-hate. This is a truth that has not been sufficiently understood by Christian writers in the past. Jesus said we must love our neighbour as ourselves. He expected us to love ourselves; the problem is not the removal of self-love but the encouragement of the right kind of self-love. Grave psychological harm can be done to people who are taught to hate themselves. It causes a deeprooted insecurity and guilt which will vitiate a man's relations with everyone he meets. Because he hates himself and cannot forgive himself for being what he is, he will unconsciously tend to put things right in his encounters with other people. He will always be trying to 'prove' himself (to himself chiefly) in his relations with others, and this can take the form of being excessively aggressive or excessively ingratiating, depending on his temperament. Whether it takes these or other forms, the point is that because the man has no value in his own eyes he will perpetually be trying to use his relationships with others to gain this value for himself. In this way selfless love of others becomes impossible. The remedy is the Christian command to love ourselves and be convinced of our own value as a unique son of God. Starting with that we can go out to love others without any distortion. This is the primary way in which charity begins at home. Only the man who loves himself is capable of loving others. Christianity's task is to see that it is the right sort of love in each case.

So far in this chapter we have discussed the problem of love for the world in terms of individualistic morality: loving other men and self. But the Christian task is by no means over when that is seen to. It is, in fact, the unbalanced concentration on individualistic Christian living in the past five hundred years in Christendom which has been a major betrayal of the gospel in modern times. The Christian is committed to a social, *political,* morality. To contract out of this duty in favour of a purely private goodness is to escape from the full demands of Christ. The Spirit has been given to us to renew the world and this demands not only personally upright dealings with our neighbour but also a commitment to the renewal of society as such. A change of heart is needed and is the fruit of life in Christ, but it must be a change of heart which does not remain in the heart but leads a man to social action to promote a Christian society. It is not sufficient to be personally renewed and to love one's neighbours if at the same time one is acquiescing in social injustice and doing nothing about the politics of life. The gospel demands not only a personal adjustment to the community we live in, but also a Christianising of that community. The community has to be adjusted too. The individualistic attitude of so many of the Christians engaged in the industrial expansion of the last hundred and fifty years, who led upright Christian lives in their families but who publicly allowed and promoted un-Christian conditions and standards of life, was and is a major lapse in Christian love. The gospel in its comprehensiveness does not allow a double standard, Christianity in private and the opposite in public. In such a case, the Christianity in private, however fervent, is unreal and an escape from Christ. All that we have said, then, about personal love for our neighbour must be seen as part of the wider love for the world which involves a follower of Christ in social awareness. The personal change of heart implied by loving our neighbour in Christ should lead us to change society as well in Christ.

In using the word 'political' to describe the social commitment involved in the gospel, we do not mean party politics in the narrow sense, but rather the broad understanding that being a Christian in society means being involved in the way society, the *polis*, is run. In differing circumstances this will mean different things. On the one hand it may mean support of the *status quo*. On the other hand it may well lead men to protest and revolution. Working out a spirituality of protest and revolution is one of the tasks to which men are addressing themselves in the development of the gospel in modern times. In a short book it is only possible to refer to this development of the social dimension of Christianity. Our general conclusion for the chapter is that a balanced following of Christ means neglecting neither person-to-person love nor social commitment. Rightly undertaken, under the guidance of the Holy Spirit, the tasks are complementary and support each other. They are both part of the genuine Christian task and privilege of surrendering to the forward movement of mankind to its final consummation in Christ.

10. Commandments and Counsels

We have seen that the development of the Christ-life in a man is the development of love, the twofold love of God and men. The next question to be asked is where the commandments fit in in the pursuit of this ideal. Jesus said 'If you love me you will keep my commandments.' (Jn 14.15). Evidently he considered that keeping commandments played a part in following him. What part that is can be gathered from noticing the order of words in Christ's remark. Not 'if you keep my commandments you will love me' but 'if you love me you will keep my commandments.' Love comes first. The motive power of the Christian life does not come from keeping laws, but from love. Love is the impetus of the Christ-life. Law must not be allowed to become that impetus. Where law comes in is as a canalisation of the impetus already provided by love. We are so made that if love is not there providing the movement of religion, then law is apt to change its function and take over as the motive power, and then we no longer have the Christian way of life but legalism. Following Christ must always be a question of loving him and *then* asking what are the ways (laws) in which he wishes us to act. It is not the Christian order to follow the laws as laws by themselves and expect love to come later. Love comes first springing from the reception of the good news of redemption – God loves us so we love him back. Law comes second as the expression of that love – we show our love for God by doing what he wants us to do.

It will be seen that in Christianity love and law go together and need each other. Love needs law. It is true that a general law can never cover the whole of an individual situation – there are elements in every situation which are unique and have to be taken into account. Nevertheless law can lay down the principles that define the general pattern of human action – like 'murder is wrong', 'marriage is indissoluble' – and so be the norm for all occasions. This is because there are for human beings such things as morally right and wrong ways of acting, though the actual area of certainty about them may be more limited than we think. In other words, law is the 'brains' of love because it provides clear norms for showing our love of God and men which are culled from studying man and from divine revelation. By applying the law to the movement of love in a given situation (which incidentally is not easy in a complex, pluralist society) we ensure that the direction our love takes is in accordance with the objective will of God – and that is the primary aim for anyone who loves. However much we grow in love we never outgrow the need for law, simply because we never outgrow the situations for which law provides the norms. As long as we are human and are in human situations, we will need the guidance of laws to help show us the way to love God. What does happen with growth in love is that following the laws becomes as it were natural to us and easier, as our mind begins to march in step with God's. This is the meaning behind the remark of St John that 'there is no fear in love but perfect love casts out fear' (1 Jn 4.18). Love does not drive out law but fear, i.e. the burden of receiving commands which go against our inclinations. As we grow in love we do not discard lawful ways of acting; on the contrary we become more law-abiding. What we discard is the immature attitude to law which sees it as a burden and an obstacle to freedom.

Equally it is obvious that law needs love. As we said

above, law is meant to be the canalisation of love, and so if love is not there we have channels without anything to channel. This is the menace of legalism: people observing laws just because they are laws without any higher motive, and so bringing about a complete alteration of the situation which law is brought in to assist. Laws are given us to guide our love of God. When love has died or is not yet born, keeping the law is a godless activity. This is what happens too often in institutional religion. It is rightly recognised as the negation of Christianity, precisely because it is the alteration of Christ's command from 'if you love me keep my commandments' to 'keep my commandments even though you do not love me or even as a substitute for loving me.' Jesus' battle with the Pharisees was over this very point. In every age of the Church a similar battle has to be fought to prevent the marrow of the Christian life being squeezed out from the bones of the Institution.

We saw that the Christ-life was a life of twofold love – of God and men. The Ten Commandments canalise these two movements. The first three specify how men must love God, and the last seven specify how they must love themselves and their neighbour. Thus the rather bleak directives of the Decalogue are in fact only a breakdown of Jesus' warmer command to love God with our whole hearts and our neighbour as ourselves. It should be noted, too, that although the commandments are worded negatively, they are actually positive, because they outlaw negative actions. In fact they enjoin the utmost love of God and neighbour, and effectively ensure that the whole of life is governed and dominated by the love of God. By exercising his love according to the commandments a man can become perfect in the following of Christ.

Is it sufficient for our love of God to have the Commandments as norms, or, if we wish to go the whole way in following Christ, must we also observe the 'counsels of perfection'? This is a question which aggravated people in the last century because they tended to answer 'yes'. By answering 'yes', they ensured that there grew up two classes of Christian: those who merely observed the commandments and could be called second-class Christians, and those who also observed the counsels of perfection (poverty, chastity, obedience and many lesser pious practices) and were first-class. Given the nineteenth-century situation of Christian withdrawal from the world, it was easy to go on from this to say that only monks and nuns or their lay imitators were first-class Christians aiming at sanctity, while the rest were second-class aiming 'merely' at salvation. The error behind this way of thinking lies in taking observance of commands and counsels as primary whereas we have seen that love is primary and observances secondary.

Christianity offers to all a way of salvation which is also that of sanctity, viz., to 'love the Lord your God with all your heart and with all your soul and with all your mind and with all your strength,... and your neighbour as yourself' (Mk 12.30-1). This is open to everyone whatever his vocation and situation in life, and (apart from the commandments, which are for all because they cater for the basic actions of life) the *way* in which each individual works out his love for God and men inevitably differs from everyone else's because no two lives are the same. This means that there is no universal secondary norm for Christian living like monasticism, but only the primary norm of the commandments. We may put this in another way by saying that there is one basic 'spirituality' which is neither monastic, priestly or lay but simply Christian, and it is for each individual to work out the details for himself. It could well be that for an individual a particular 'counsel of perfection' was necessary in order to preserve or promote his following of Christ in a given situation (e.g. fasting), but this is not the same as saying that the counsels of perfection are always necessary. In this way it is seen more clearly that all are called to follow Christ to the end (which is salvation-sanctity) and that to do this only the commandments are universally obligatory. In other words there is a 'universal call to holiness' which is given to man at baptism along with the gifts of the Holy Spirit and grace which help him answer that call. If he is a priest the way in which he answers this call will naturally differ from the way in which a layman answers it, but neither one nor the other is a higher way. All Christians belong to one unique Way which is the highest of all.

11. *Self-Denial*

We saw in Chapter 9 that because the Christ-life means loving men, and because in us all there is a tendency to misdirect this love to selfish purposes, poverty of spirit is an essential element in Christian development. Poverty of spirit is not doing without things (which is self-denial) but having things in a spirit of detachment. It is loving without possessiveness. If we do not make a positive effort to achieve this the life of grace will not grow in us, but will be stifled in self-love. In other words the spirit of poverty has a central place in Christian living. It is not something added to the love of men commanded by Christ, but the built-in safeguard and condition of that love. Without it love does not dwell in a man, but only possessiveness, and all he does, even his religious acts, will turn to self-advancement. Poverty of spirit, then, belongs to the essence of the Christ-life. What part, if any, does self-denial play? Is it an essential, or merely an optional extra practised by those who feel inclined towards monastic observances?

Self-denial was not made central by Christ. He commanded love – the outward-going movement of man in society towards God and his neighbour. But in so far as self-denial is something that helps us to love, then it is a good thing. Because of original sin we are prone to turn our actions into self-love, and even make religion serve our self-regarding needs. When this happens what is needed is an action or series of actions which turn us away from ourselves disciplining us to conquer self-love and go outwards to our neighbour. By saying 'no' to ourselves we can train ourselves to say 'yes' to other people more readily. The saying of 'no' to ourselves is self-denial. In theory it is conceivable that a man will concentrate on loving without the need of self-denial. But in practice it is good to train ourselves to love by deliberately denying ourselves legitimate satisfactions. The point is that self-denial must never become an end in itself but only a means to love, for love is the purpose of Christian living. If this is remembered, then self-denial falls into place and does not become more important than the central actions of loving our neighbour and worshipping God. We are not required by Christ to give up any of the things of this world which are all good and in no way evil; nevertheless we do deny ourselves the pleasure and possession of legitimate good things in order to train ourselves to have what we have in poverty of spirit. Possessions are not bad in themselves but in practice we need self-denial to help us handle them properly. By doing without *some* things we ensure, with God's grace, that we possess *all* things in poverty of spirit. Doing without things is not the aim of Christian living but it has proved a powerful means of making sure that we possess what we do possess with selflessness as stewards of the Lord.

There is a long and respectable tradition in the Church for self-denial. It starts with Jesus himself who fasted in the desert and went without comfort in order to equip himself for his mission more aptly. Less than any man did he have to fast, but he did so, as well as on other occasions feasting. Both the feasting and the fasting were parts of his mission to love all men his brothers. We have a good description of the place of self-denial in the Christian life in Lk 13.6-9:

And he told them this parable: A man had a fig tree planted in his vineyard; and he came seeking fruit on it and found none. And he said to the vinedresser, 'Lo, these three years I have come seeking fruit on this fig tree, and I find none. Cut it down; why should it use up the ground?' And he answered him, 'Let it alone, sir, this year also, till I dig it about and put on manure. And if it bears fruit next year, well and good; but if not, you can cut it down.'

The way to see self-denial in the Christian scheme of things is as the pruning of the fruit-tree that every good gardener undertakes in order to improve the harvest. St Paul's image was of the athlete who submits himself to rigorous discipline in order to run more effectively and win the race.

Do you not know that in a race all the runners compete, but only one receives the prize? So run that you may obtain it. Every athlete exercises self-control in all things. They do it to receive a perishable wreath, but we an imperishable one. Well, I do not run aimlessly, I do not box as one beating the air; but I pommel my body and subdue it, lest after preaching to others I myself should be disqualified (1 Cor 9.24-27).

These images express in their own way a truth that is part of human wisdom, and not specially connected with religion, that all growth demands loss as well as gain, a narrowing in one area of life in order to achieve a broadening in the whole. No man develops towards maturity without renouncing pleasures and training himself in self-discipline. The particular Christian contribution to this is that it is done for the overall motive of conforming us to Christ.

There is, therefore, a further dimension added by Christ to voluntary suffering. This is the opportunity it affords as part of a Christian's participation in the paschal mystery. In this sense it is an overflow of love rather than a preparation for it. Jesus assured his disciples that following him involved taking up the cross. In saying this he was not introducing an element (suffering) into their lives which was alien to ordinary human life, but pointing out the way in which he wanted his followers to handle this already basic human experience, viz., by voluntarily accepting it for his sake. Taking up the cross can mean two things: either the voluntary self-denial we have been outlining so far in this chapter, done for Christ's sake, or the acceptance of suffering which comes from events and people outside ourselves, also for Christ's sake. The latter is in fact a more potent factor in Christian development than voluntary self-denial because it obviates the danger of self-inflation which is present in all self-imposed mortifications.

> Truly, truly, I say to you, when you were young, you girded yourself and walked where you would; but when you are old, you will stretch out your hands, and another will gird you and carry you where you do not wish to go (Jn 21.18).

There is a closer assimilation to Christ in the voluntary acceptance of suffering than in self-imposed renunciation, but both are Christian actions when they are done for Jesus Christ. All human growth involves accepting suffering and making it fruitful; what Jesus did was to identify this universal human struggle with his own acceptance of the cross, so that for Christians it is no longer an impersonal act done for themselves but a deeply personal participation in the mystery of Christ's redemption.

To sum up we may say that self-denial is a necessary

evil owing to the fact of original sin and the consequent fatal tendency of man to attach himself in the wrong way to creatures. It is not an end in itself but a painful means towards a greater good: the pruning of the fruit tree by the gardener. Self-denial is death to self in one department of life but only in order to bring greater life to the whole. Like Jesus' death it leads to resurrection. Our participation in the paschal mystery is a share in the death of Christ only in order to lead us to share in his resurrection and glory (cf. Rom 6.3-11).

We sometimes fear that self-denial is repression of a natural instinct and therefore psychologically dangerous. It is as well to be clear that this is not so. The self-denial we have been talking about amounts psychologically to suppression, not repression. There is a difference between the two: *Repression* is an involuntary running away from a situation, a preconscious failure to face up to the frequently ugly truth about one's instincts. An instinctive defence-mechanism, it is resisting evil by denying one's involvement in it, brushing it under the carpet. This causes psychological trouble, because we cannot pretend that we have no involvement in evil. It can be dismissed from the conscious mind, but it remains as an unsolved problem in the unconscious mind, and may later erupt as a neurosis. *Suppression* is a conscious, volitional choice, in accordance with the dictates of reason. This means facing up to the truth about one's ugly instincts and doing something about them by consciously resisting the evil in them. It is of course frequently a painful and difficult choice to make and may cause conflict and suffering, but it does not cause neurosis. As we have seen, all growth to maturity involves some degree of suppression. One of the ways in which we do this is by self-denial.

PART III

The Development of the Christian Response

In Parts I and II of this book we have examined the pattern of spirituality created by the dogmatic facts of God's self-revelation in Christ. In this third part we 'begin at the other end' and examine how the personal development of a Christian grows from within himself.

12. Beginnings

'All real living is meeting,' said Martin Buber. We live and grow by relating to ourselves and to things and people outside ourselves. The whole of life is thus a confrontation – with our own selves, others and eventually God. These successive confrontations either develop or diminish our personalities; there is no remaining still. For the baptised Christian each of these meetings is in addition an encounter with Christ resulting in his growth or diminishment in the Christ-life as an adopted son of the Father.

(1) *Relating to Self*

First of all we meet ourselves. Each succeeding confrontation of life, whether it be with things or with people, is also a confrontation with self. We learn to know, love and control ourselves in dialogue with others. If we are earnest and honest in this pursuit we will become mature in our humanity. Maturity can be described as having emotional control, self-knowledge and true love of self. In dealing with our emotions we have to avoid the two aberrations of treating them as subhuman and dangerous and of regarding them as the whole of ourselves. Neither of these positions is correct. The heart must not control the head nor must it in turn be repressed by the head. True humanity consists in realising that our emotions *are* ourselves – when we love or hate or are afraid it is we who are reacting like this with the whole of ourselves and we are blind if we pretend otherwise. Nevertheless these emotional drives by which we express ourselves are in need of control from the head without which they are pilotless. They must, as it were, pass in every situation from being merely automatic responses to being the authentic course of action we decide to take. They need direction which does not diminish their fire but takes it up and uses it. This direction can either take the form of encouraging or suppressing the initial emotional reaction. Rational love sometimes asks for passionate action and sometimes for tranquillity. But in neither case is the emotional response repressed (cf. page 75).

Christians can go further than non-believers and see in this human development the imitation of Jesus Christ, whose emotional life was a full-blooded but well-ordered use of his passions. Being angry with the Pharisees, weeping at Lazarus's tomb, sweating with fear in Gethsemane, remaining silent at his trial – in all these situations Jesus showed that he was an authentic human person, who neither repressed his human passions nor allowed them to control him. In each case there is a hidden power in his emotional outbursts manifesting a harmony between heart and head. Christians, with their doctrine and experience of original sin, realise that this harmony is not an easily acquired state but the fruit of toil. This is where the practice of self-denial at the start of the Christian life comes in (Chapter 11). By voluntarily giving up emotional and sensual pleasures which in themselves are innocent, we train ourselves to have control in those passionate areas of life. We go without food and drink (fasting), sleep (vigils), money (almsgiving). To these traditional practices we can add any number of deprivations which help us not to be ruled by our immediate needs regardless of our long-term ones. The mortification of the automatic reactions of curiosity, impatience, laziness, time-wasting and similar reflexes is a fruitful way to gain a lasting control over ourselves. There is little growth in the Christian life without those diminishments.

Emotional control demands self-knowledge as its complement. This is the second primary task of the beginner. Life forces self-knowledge upon us, and it is essential that we have the courage to face it and not run away. All too easily we turn away because self-knowledge is reality dawning upon us and 'human kind cannot bear very much reality' (T. S. Eliot). The genuinely developed human person is the one who has received with tranquillity both the good and bad revelations of his character that successive situations in life have presented to him and has made that knowledge part of himself. In this matter of self-knowledge we can only at first be expected to have knowledge of our conscious selves, but conscientious self-examination will lead us to knowledge of our unconscious selves too, at least in the non-technical sense that we know our temperamental biases (conformist/non-conformist, extravert/introvert etc.) and can spot the more obvious rationalisations and escapes that result from them. This does not presuppose an intelligent or sophisticated individual. It is a question of honesty rather than cleverness, and uneducated people sometimes prove that they know themselves at this level better than more educated ones, even though they may not be able to articulate their knowledge. Such introversion, however, should not become morbid pre-occupation with self, because that destroys the whole object of self-examination, which is to equip us to go out to other people and love them more readily. This is why help from others in the form of counsel is desirable, because other people are quick to prevent us becoming preoccupied with self, and also because they provide a more objective account of ourselves than we can give ourselves. This counsel can be provided either by an individual or by a group. Those who have taken part in group *revisions de vie* have found the communal appraisal of the individual to be both helpful and healthy.

It is, however, no good knowing the truth about ourselves, that we are prone to this or that bad action and capable of this or that good one, without doing something about it. Everyone must react existentially to his self-knowledge, otherwise he remains merely academic. For the Christian this commitment to doing something about himself is not merely a question of the perfection of self (it is that), but also of pleasing God. In other words we have not only to know ourselves and commit ourselves in all the relationships of life but also we must make this commitment a personal reaction in Christ. To use the terminology of gospel enquiries, the See and the Judge about ourselves have to be followed by an Act, which is at one level a reaction to a human situation and at another level a personal reaction to God the Father. Thus knowledge of self leads to the pursuit of morality, and *vice versa*.

When we judge that our actions have been bad, we judge that they are sins, and then the personal reaction is sorrow to God. Being sorry for our sins and determining to do something about them is one of the primary actions of the Christian conscience. As we saw in Chapter 8, it is an inevitable fruit of the approach to God in prayer, and without it Christian growth is illusory. 'If we say we have no sin, we deceive ourselves, and the truth is not in us' (1 Jn 1.8). Two simple distinctions have to be made here. First, we must distinguish between feeling sorry and being sorry for our sins. The latter is what matters, a turning away of the whole person from sin. Sometimes it is accompanied by feelings of sorrow which greatly help, but these feelings are not necessary to genuine sorrow. Genuine sorrow is wishing we had not done a certain act and resolving not to do it again. It is a conversion of the mind. The only real proof of its validity is the effort to reform by taking positive steps to do better. (Whether these efforts succeed or not is beside the point). Feelings of sorrow are not always indicative of this resolve, though at times they may be helpful in producing it. The second distinction that has to be made is not unconnected with the one before. It is the distinction between remorse – sorrow for sin because of the harm it does to ourselves, wounded pride in fact – and real sorrow which is on account of the failure to please God. The former is self-centred, the latter God-centred. On the night of the Passion Judas felt remorse for his act and went off by himself to die without God, while Peter was overcome by genuine sorrow and came back to Jesus.

(2) *Relating to Others*

Our self-knowledge and commitment does not take place in a vacuum. We relate to other people at the same time as we relate to ourselves. There is no space here to outline all the possible ways in which men relate to each other. This is not necessary, however, because all the variations of human relationship depend upon one fundamental one: our basic attitude towards the Other. We grow in our humanity if we adopt an open attitude towards other people, ready to take the risk of going out to them, to be 'decentralised', take root in them; in a nutshell, *love* them. Conversely, we diminish in humanity if we close up, run away from being committed to others, see the risks involved as too great and remain shut and turned in on ourselves, 'centralised' on self. This is the fundamental option of our lives and boils down to whether we love other people or hate them. All the various prescriptions of the codes of human behaviour are expansions of that fundamental attitude of openness towards the Other. To be honest, caring, generous, just, chaste, truthful and so on is merely to be loving towards other men and towards society in particular situations. A man's fundamental option determines the course of his moral action, and good moral action is the result of relating to others in an open and loving way. Hence the obstacles in us to being open and loving to the Other are the roots of immoral actions or sins. Sin is precisely being turned in on self and away from others in particular situations, and it leads to being dishonest, selfish, malicious, unjust, impure, untruthful, as the case may be. The root of all sin is that fear in us of being committed, the innate desire to remain shut within ourselves, the refusal to take root in the not-I. This desire is deep in us all. It is the root of all sins, being a propensity planted in us – original sin, rather than actually a sin itself. The wise man, therefore, will be watchful of this more than any actual immorality because it is the foundation of all sinning, the Pride which is behind and beneath each of the seven deadly sins.

From the Christian point of view this movement to be open towards the Other is the movement of the Spirit within us. It purifies us from desire to remain shut, which is Pride. The Spirit from the depths of our being says 'yes' to the Other and drives us to go out in love to everyone we meet. As Christians, therefore, we have two aids: externally the example of the life of Christ, whose fundamental achievement was precisely this loving concern for others, and internally the life of this same Risen Christ which penetrates and elevates our natural love. Both 'hands' of God point the same way to love.

As we noted in Chapter 9, loving others is not only a question of individuals loving individuals. It is also a communal preoccupation, for the Spirit is given to the Church to renew the face of the earth, to uproot unjust government and purify the social structures we live with. Hence a very important part of this relating to others in Christ is our commitment to society as a whole. By being responsibly aware of the society we live in – and ultimately the society we live in is the whole of mankind, so there are no limits – we fulfil our Christian vocation. This means suppressing the urge to be socially uncommitted (a variation of the refusal to take root in the Other) and playing a part in the renewal of society. As has been already noted, this may point to revolutionary action at times, for if the personal obstacles to charity are individual blocks like pride and laziness, the communal obstacles are the external barriers so often written into the structures of society like barriers of race, colour, class, privilege, creed. These can sometimes only be removed violently. It is as much a work of charity to do this as to work away at our personal sins in private life. True development demands both kinds of growth in love, the individual and the social.

(3) *Relating to God*

Finally we relate to God. Just as the relationship we have towards ourselves and others are not separable but intermingled – we 'meet' ourselves in meeting people – so *a fortiori* our relationship to God is not a separate action performed at a different time from all the rest of our human acts but is a particular dimension to the everyday actions of life. God is in the world and the world is in God. Hence we 'meet' God and relate to him within the secular relationships we have in the world. The two obligations of loving God and loving men (discussed in Chapters 8 and 9) are not separate actions but separate facets of the one Christian endeavour in life. We encounter God within the encounters of life, and *vice versa* we encounter our fellow men in the act of praying to God. Life and prayer are not directed towards men and God respectively but are each directed to both men and God. This is best seen in the public liturgy of the Church, which is a communal act (even when apparently private, as in confession). The body of the Church as well as God is involved. Participating in the liturgy we encounter men and God simultaneously.

The sacraments which are most relevant at this stage in

the Christian life are those of Confession and the Eucharist. By the sacrament of Confession our efforts to examine self, confess our sins and be converted back to God (which we examined at the beginning of this chapter) are taken up and identified with Christ's unique and victorious war against sin (cf. Chapter 5). In the same way the individual's effort to go out from self in love to his neighbour and to God (which we examined secondly in this chapter) are assumed into the great movement of the love of the Son for the Father in the sacrament of the Eucharist. Participating along with his fellow Christians in the Body of Christ, the individual is given the grace of Christ to revise his life and make it pleasing to God. Holy Communion both symbolises and strengthens with divine power the Christian effort to do good and love God and men. It is the most potent of all the elements in the struggle to break out of our basic imprisonment within the self and convert our lives into genuine openness towards the needs of others. Under the influence of the Eucharist our baptismal union with God in being develops into a dynamic union of Christian behaviour (cf. Chapter 5).

This gathering up of the whole of the Christian effort – examination of self, pursuit of morality, love – into liturgical prayer should overflow into personal prayer. The various relationships of life, to self and to others, can explicitly be made part of our underlying relationship to God. When this happens we have personal prayer. The wise man sets aside time to do this and does not merely rely on an implicit depth-relationship to God within his other relationships. It is, of course, true that that depth-relationship is there always (de Caussade's 'sacrament of the present moment'), but this needs explicit reflecting upon, especially by beginners. When we do this we pray. Prayer is saying 'yes' to God as the expression of the Yes of our whole life.

There are two approaches to prayer, and which of them is initially adopted depends largely on the temperament of the man who prays. Either we begin with God and his revelation and ponder upon it in a way which throws light on our life and relationships to others, or we begin by pondering upon a situation in life and from there approach to God by judging it in the light of his nature and plan of redemption. The first way means starting with the Bible or some book which derives from it. The incident on page 27 describing Dr Orchard's grandfather meditatively reading the New Testament is an example of this sort of prayer which has supported countless Christians through the ages; the Y.C.W. Gospel Enquiry is a modern example of the practice. The second way of praying has an appeal to modern men who are anxious to situate their Christian response right in the middle of their ordinary lives. It consists in spending time reflecting on life, either in general or in a particular incident, under the light of God's redeeming love. The *Prayers of Life* of Michel Quoist are good examples of this 'praying from life', as also is the Y.C.W. Social Enquiry. In all this the important thing is to join ourselves, other people and God together in our hearts in prayer, so that whichever end we begin from, Revelation or Life, we end up with a comprehensive mutual relationship of self, world and God in the act of prayer. The Our Father is the best expression of this comprehensive way of praying, but acts of faith, hope, charity or contrition for sins can all be prayed in this way. Prayer like this has a unifying effect on our lives, and unity is the work of God.

13. Crisis

The Christian life in the individual is essentially a growth. This means that it will have crises of growth through which progress comes. We have Jesus' parable of the sower and the seed and the fate of the seed which sprang up with no roots to remind us that the first crisis of growth in any human undertaking is concerned with the striking of roots firmly into the ground to provide sufficient basis for future growing. This is true of the growth of the Christ-life as much as any other kind of human maturing. For some time after the decision to take seriously the claims of the Christian life, as opposed to merely fitting in with one's cultural environment, there exists in all of us a joy and a zest in spirituality which is as natural as the joy and zest we experience after beginning any worthwhile venture. But soon in its wake there follows an evaporation of the original zest. This is the crisis of growth, when the roots of our Christian spirituality are struck or not, as the case may be.

This first crisis takes the form of a growing disillusionment in the three relationships which form the Christ-life: to God, to others and to self. The disillusionment in our relationship to God manifests itself most acutely in prayer. Prayer becomes dry and apparently meaningless. Formulas that used to mean much to us, books and people who inspired us to greater efforts, places which helped us to pray well, all these tend to lose their significance. We feel that nothing now holds much meaning and are greatly tempted to stop praying. If we keep on praying, our prayer is full of distracting thoughts which seem to separate us from God. It is the same with the pursuit of morality and the avoidance of sin. Here too the campaign of going out to others in love and conquering our radical urge not to be involved is apt to 'go dead' on us. This disillusion with our own attempts to love is equalled by a parallel disillusion with the 'lovability' of other people; their faults and failings show up with considerably more clarity than before we tried to love them. Finally this disenchantment spreads to our relations with self, and we begin to see ourselves as apparently going backwards spiritually, with more faults as we progress rather than less. We are thoroughly dissatisfied with the 'I' that appears in the centre of all we do. Whereas we expected our progress in the spiritual life to accelerate and lead us to more insights into the Christian Mystery, our experience tends to be the opposite – less understanding of the Christ-life and less love. To anyone who has tried hard to please God and lead a Christian life this early check to his commitment is difficult to bear, for it seems to make a mockery of his efforts.

The way we react to this situation of disillusion is crucial to our development. The boredom which comes upon us is in fact an instrument of further spiritual advance even though it feels like spiritual retreat. It depends on how we react. The right way to react is simply to persevere. If we do this maturity will be our reward. By carrying on without any of the former emotional returns we prove to ourselves (and to God) that we do not need surface consolations in the life of the spirit, but are engaged for deeper and more lasting motives. Thus a radical purification of motive takes place if we persevere in the trial. Deprived of the former superficial and inadequate motives for praying and leading the Christian life, we are forced to dredge up from within ourselves deeper and truer motives. We can no longer pray because of consolations – they have gone; nor can we mortify ourselves for the satisfaction of knowing it to be worthwhile – we begin to doubt that; nor can we love people for the feeling that we are of use to them – that feeling has disappeared. Why, then, do we carry on? The reason, we gradually discern, is that all the time we have had a more valid motive which was hidden beneath the more superficial ones, viz. we want to please God. Prayer, self-denial, moral actions are now being done because they serve God not self. Our love is being turned inside out from the love that looks for spiritual self-advantage, the love that takes, to the love that looks to serve God, the love that gives. This is, of course, a gradual process and does not take place with the speed or the facility that a simple description of it might suggest. It is for most people a painful progress through bewilderment, failure and defeat. It is easy to write about it from the point of view of an objective observer, but when it happens to a particular individual that individual does not readily recognise it as a process of spiritual purification, but is more likely to be merely surprised and hurt. This is part of the disillusionment. If we knew that trials came from the loving hand of God they would not really be trials.

Disillusionment about self and religion should result in a greatly increased maturity in the Christian life. The deflating sight of self as mediocre and weak and not going forward makes us on the one hand more diligent at the Christian task and on the other more humble and actively dependent on help from God (not only in our 'weakness' but also in our 'strength', which is now seen as itself dependent on God). The result of these realisations is a greater depth of Christianity: the man who knows existentially that he needs God in everything he does is closer to Christ than the self-confident beginner whose confidence is illusory. The mature Christian is the one who has learnt to live with the knowledge that he is weak and helpless without grace and yet does not give in to despair at this knowledge. He knows it to be the truth – it is really true that he is a sinner and cannot by himself please God – and because he knows this he is living in the light of reality and can rejoice. The one who is not living in a real world is the beginner who has not yet gone through the bitter trial of disenchantment with religion. In our Lord's parable about the Pharisee and the Publican in the temple, the Pharisee was living in a dream-world of spiritual success, while the Publican was living in the real world with no illusions about himself. In other words, the trials we have been describing make us face reality. That is why they can be described as leading to maturity, for the important feature of maturity in personality-development is that it is a facing of reality. Children live of necessity in a world of illusions – about themselves, their parents, other people – a romantic world removed from reality and full of comforting escapes. Growing up for them means the gradual learning of the truth about themselves and others, closing the doors one by one to escapes from this lesson. The trial we have been outlining does the same for the Christian. It brings him nearer to the truth about life, understood in the light not only of a growing knowledge of the world but also in the light of God and his eternal plan of salvation.

In terms of Jungian psychology what we have been describing is the first step in psychological maturity, viz., the integration of a man's *shadow* with his *persona*. Our shadow is the reality of the unacknowledged evil in us; our persona is the ideal and artificial figure we make for ourselves which we unconsciously act out before the audience of life (including ourselves); it is essentially an escape role. Maturity comes when we acknowledge the evil within us as a real part of ourselves (make our shadow part of our conscious life), and recognise that the artificial public figure we act out before people is in fact artificial (make our persona part of our conscious life). In other words we become real not false about ourselves. It is precisely this which the experience of disillusion in the serious following of Christ produces in us – the integration of our sinfulness with our ideals so as to make a balanced whole based on reality.

From this cleansed vision of our self without illusion there follows a cleansed vision of the rest of men. We can only make a true judgment about other people after we have achieved a true judgment about ourselves. Before, our vision is biased, but afterwards, we know the biases and have clear sight. As Jesus noticed, we must remove the log in our own eye before proceeding with the specks in others'.

Having faithfully faced the reality about ourselves and other people, the next step is to react with the same fidelity. This means resisting the temptation to despair which is liable to afflict someone who is learning the truth about himself in the penetrating light of God. Reacting with reality for a Christian means acknowledging the goodness and mercy of the Father and so running to him for pardon. This is the message of Jesus' parable of the Prodigal Son. The Prodigal Son went through the experience of being stripped of illusions about himself and was brought face to face with reality. Then he remembered that reality included his father's love for him and went back home with confidence knowing that he would be taken back. When we have been through the painful process of seeing ourselves in the light of reality, we also have to remember the whole picture which includes the fact that God is a loving Father and Jesus Christ our Saviour. This will prompt us to come humbly but courageously to the decision not to despair but to repent of our sins and return to God. It is the difference once more between Judas and Peter on the night of the Passion, between sterile remorse and creative sorrow.

The process of disillusion and stripping which we undergo in going to God is the antidote to the perennial danger of religious people – making religion serve the glorification of self not God. This is the peril of pharisaism, the fatal tendency the best of us has to use his religion to inflate his own importance. When someone undertakes the spiritual campaigns of love, self-examination and prayer, and achieves a measure of tangible success as a result of his zeal, the danger is that he will grow in self-importance. He begins to feel he is doing well, better in fact than other people. From that it is but a step to becoming intolerant of others and supercilious about their efforts. The final result is a man who has a high opinion of himself and a low one of others in the name of religion. The way to prevent this happening is for religion itself to have a deflating effect on man, and the only way for this to come about is for low esteem of self rather than high esteem to be the outcome of spiritual effort. But of course the failure of spiritual effort is only relative, viz. failure on the part of man unaided by God, not failure with God, who enables us to 'do all things'. The outcome of this crisis of growth in spirituality is in fact the realisation that although of ourselves we are mediocre and prone to evil, with the grace of God and in him alone we can do all things. The crisis leads to optimism not pessimism, to a confident commitment to the task of living the Christian life, not a pessimistic withdrawal. This is the meaning of grace, the divinisation of man. The crisis of growth in the Christian life in the last analysis is merely the experience of grace in the soul. As we saw in Chapter 5 it is bound to be a passover experience, a passage to life through death, because all grace is union with Jesus Christ in his Passover. It is to be expected, then, that growth in the grace of Christ will involve the Christian in suffering before he enters into glory (cf. Lk 24.26).

14. Growth in Christ

If properly understood and accepted, the crisis described in the last chapter is a liberation from complexity for the person who undergoes it. The increased realisation of ourselves as dependent on God in our spiritual growth has the effect of making us centre our lives more on the simplicity of God and less on the complexity of our own efforts. We begin to find God more where he truly is, in the centre of our being and relationships, and we emerge with a new psychological unity in our Christian lives. The purpose of this chapter is to give a brief description of this psychological unification. The various simplifications which occur at this stage in the life of grace are not an abandonment of previous Christian duties, but merely an alteration of method in performing them. Friends dispense with the fuss and bother of initial courtesies towards each other as they grow in friendship; such a change is not a cooling off of their friendship but a simplification of procedure which actually manifests greater warmth and union than the earlier punctiliousness. The best model for growth in the Christ-life is to describe it as a growth in friendship between self and God, the creation of an I-Thou relationship between ourselves and God, which we saw in Chapter 6 was the purpose of God's self-giving in grace. It is therefore to be expected that spiritual growth will manifest a similar simplification of procedure between the soul and God.

Our relationship to God in prayer is the centre of focus of this simplification. In whatever way we prayed up to now – whether by reflecting on the Bible and theology or by reflecting on incidents in life, or both, which is more balanced – our prayer begins to become more simple. The act of reflection itself becomes easier because more familiar. It needs less discourse and becomes more intuitive, as all familiarly repeated acts do. In turn the response which follows that reflecting upon God and life becomes simpler, less a series of articulated acts and more a unified response of love. This, too, becomes intuitive and less discursive; familiarity has led to simplicity and ease. Thus, in our moments of prayer we find ourselves thinking with greater ease and assurance about the manifold complexities of life, seeing it all as a unity and responding to this unified view with corresponding simplicity. Such prayer can rightly be called contemplative because self, others and God are now apprehended in one 'gaze' rather than experienced separately and then related laboriously together. It is not that we have made the relationships of life come together in a unity, but that we begin to see with a new clarity the unity that already exists between them. We no longer want to speak of three relationships in life: to self, others and God. We prefer now to call them three facets of the one relationship. In the first place, it is not possible to mark off boundaries where our relationship to self ends and that to others begins, because we establish our relationship to self in relating to others, and *vice versa*. Above all we begin to see that the profound reality which is God penetrates every moment and corner of our lives, because in him we live and move and have our being, so that it is unreal to speak of a separate relationship to God in life when the whole of life is bound up with God by its very existence. De Caussade coined the phrase 'sacrament of the present moment' to express this fact. It is in our periods of contemplative prayer that we realise the truth of this phrase most, and relinquish our times for prayer knowing that the relationship continues after we have got up from our knees. The presence of God goes with us and is discovered in the continuous sacrament of our involvement with the secular.

Many books have been written about contemplative prayer and its mechanics. In this paragraph we will only briefly outline what they say and refer the reader to them for further instruction. (See Appendix.)

(1) *The subject who prays*

In this prayer there is an awareness by the person praying that he is engaged in the depth of his soul, that the centre of gravity of his prayer has shifted from the surface of his self where his imagination dwells to a deeper part of him. At the deepest level of his being, beneath the imagination, he is in contact with God. The imagination still has to be occupied and is best given some sort of sop like a picture, a remembered phrase, darkness, silence, and so on, but the activity of prayer is conducted through and beneath it at a deeper level.

(2) *The act of prayer*

The activity of prayer itself is experienced as an activity of the whole person as he is drawn into the orbit of God's love, this activity being more in the nature of a surrender to God than any particular mental process. The mediaeval phrase 'naked intent unto God' describes well what this act is felt to be – naked of all human images and artifices, an intent of the whole person rather than a particular activity of imagination, mind or will. There is an experience of silent absorption in the reality of God, in and around and undergirding us as we pray, an overwhelming feeling of contact, not with ideas about God but with God. It is felt as a person-to-person encounter or a surrender to a personal divine field of force, depending on the model used.

(3) *The object of prayer*

Lastly the truth of the incomprehensibility of God and the fact, noted in Chapter 2, that God transcends all human modes of thought, is grasped existentially. Eventually human models have to give way in prayer and the negation of them is felt to be truer to the reality experienced than any affirmation, old or new. In the 'darkness' of this 'unknowing' there is a comprehensiveness in thinking about God which transcends all the ideas and theories of theology. At a deeper level than conceptual thought the various complementary approaches to thinking about God converge and meet in a living experience of the whole self engaged with God. This experience is felt to be one of silence, not speech, in which the mind and heart of man remain 'beaten' but perfectly content to be so in faith. Any attempt to make a model of this experience of God, however refined, is known to be self-defeating. God is always beyond the last image that is made of him; plates of the purest gold hide him as effectively as the beginner's plates of iron.

It is a mistake to think that it is only during periods of prayer that we experience this deep and simple relationship to God. It can be experienced at any moment in life, because in every moment of life we are in contact with this ineffable God. In fact, one of the features of this deepening of the spiritual life is the awareness that the whole of life is becoming a prayer. The other relationships of life have become penetrated with the presence of God. The specific activities (cf. Chapter 12) of examination of self, pursuit of morality and overall love of our neighbour become penetrated with the presence of God, and are performed as personal encounters with the Father in Christ. Thus, the avoidance of sin passes from being an examination of particular activities of the self to being a simple effort to please God; it is not individual sins or habits of sin which stand out as obstacles to Christian living but the radical sinfulness in us which is our refusal to be open to God. We are overcome by a desire to confess our sinfulness, or Sin, rather than particular sins, and the horror of Sin afflicts us with increasing strength. Again, the pursuit of virtue simplifies into a pursuit of the love of neighbour and God. We pursue virtue at source and do not bother much about the multifarious actions of life, categorised under headings corresponding to this or that virtue. Pleasing God, whom we love in Christ, is our aim now. The whole of life becomes prayer to the Father. It is a personal relationship to the world in Christ and through the world to God, and attempts to depersonalise it in terms of virtues and vices are seen as inadequate and misleading.

Summing up this chapter, we may say that growth of intimacy in the Christian life results in four shifts of emphasis in our approach to our neighbour and God. To begin with, there is a shift of emphasis within man away from concentration on his emotional responses towards a deeper level of human living in which the whole man is engaged, often without emotional assistance. Looking after a sick person, for instance, is not accompanied by passion or excitement; something deeper is its steady driving-force. This shift of emphasis is accompanied by an evolution from complexity to simplicity. As we noted above, the underlying unity of all we do and are in life springs into prominence as a Christian gains confidence in his approach to life. That love which is a steady driving-force is essentially a simple thing and does not need complexity to draw it out or sustain it. A third shift of emphasis is found to consist in a deepening of Christian action. It would be wrong to call this bluntly a change of emphasis from doing to being, though properly understood that phrase expresses it well. It is not that we cease to act or go out to our neighbour in love and choose to be inactive and pray. That is the error of the Quietists who thought that union with God was synonymous with rest and so adulterated the gospel. What happens in genuine Christian development is that the activity of our lives, which normally increases as our involvement in Christ does, becomes less frenzied and more tranquil. The growing realisation that our activity is in Christ and depends on his strength and not ours unaided, that we are branches of a great Vine, has the effect of releasing us from fuss and flurry and making our lives more peaceful in their activity. The busiest saints have been the mystics, and the mystics have been the busiest saints. The fourth and comprehensive change in emphasis in the Christ-life is the change from centring on self to centring on God, a turning of the whole Christian effort inside out. Life, work, activity, prayer are now done not for any motives of self-perfection or fulfilment, but simply for God. This is the change which makes the other ones understandable. Our lives begin to centre on God, and in that turning away from self, fulfilment is achieved. It is the paradox of the gospel message that we find ourselves only when we have resolutely determined to lose ourselves.

15. Towards Fulfilment

The crisis we described in Chapter 13 is a crisis centring on the emotional life of the Christian out of which emerges a measure of freedom in the use of his passions for life in the secular world. In terms of morality it is a crisis of the moral virtues, the virtues which relate a man to himself like prudence and justice even while relating him to others. Fulfilment of the life of grace, however, is not achieved without a further crisis which centres this time round the mind and will, or deepest self, in man. This crisis involves a painful detachment from our most personal instincts and operations so that they may be given over wholly to God and operate outwards to others and not inwards to self. This is basically a crisis not of morality – how should we act? – but of faith, hope and charity – what is it all about? Through it comes a purification of the deepest movements in the soul of the Christian whereby he responds to the call of his adoption by the Father. It is a time which tests the basic self in us all, the self which 'makes us tick', the profound 'I' at the root of all action. Genuine faith, hope and charity cannot be said to exist – in other words no man can be fulfilled as a son of God – until this basic 'I' has been brought under the influence of grace and made to respond instinctively away from self and towards the Other. This is the ultimate meaning of the phrase 'putting on Christ'. It means living for others, existing outwards, as Jesus Christ did.

It is a purification of loving. The immature Christian loves God and men for a mixture of motives: joy, contentment, zest in the life of the spirit, a certain deep satisfaction in contemplative prayer and involvement in mankind. These are good motives but insufficient. The most valid reason for loving God is because he is what he is! The process by which we are led to this realisation is the loss of all those secondary motives of joy and contentment in following Christ. These 'go dead', and the Christian is left trying to love God and men for no other reason than that God is God – a supremely naked state of soul out of which emerges a pure and unalloyed love of God and all men, buttressed this time not by 'spiritual' or 'religious' motives but by the plain fact of God and his mystery of salvation. In this light all 'religion' is seen as marginal to pure love and by no means the core of Christian living.

It is a purification of hoping. Here, too, immature Christians instinctively base their lives in fact if not in theory on less than the highest motives for hope. A certain confidence in self based on past success, an ease of manner, a feeling of being at home in Christianity have all helped to contribute to the confidence of the follower of Christ and keep him going. These are good but secondary elements in the Christian life. The one valid reason for hoping in God is the goodness of God himself. To learn this the Christian has to undergo a parallel death of self-confidence. He finds himself now bereft of confidence in areas where before he was at ease, with seemingly no support or friends, facing the future gloomily aware of a creeping meaninglessness in his existence. Out of this naked state of despair in secondary human supports emerges a hope, genuinely based on God, a real confidence in him, understood to be the Father, as it were for the first time.

It is a purification of believing. Faith in God and his Son is the ultimate basis for all Christian living. Like all ultimate bases it can go for years without being questioned. The average Christian depends in practice on secondary and, in the last analysis, inadequate motives for believing: the accepted beliefs of his background, a certain acceptability about the life and doctrines of the Church, an apparent experience of God's actions in his life. In the night of purification these buttresses to faith simply dissolve into thin air and the Christian is left questioning all the things he has up to then accepted, doubting their validity in a frightening sort of way. This is a crisis of his whole life, for it questions the very direction of his living. It is, in fact, the inmost dimension of the crisis whose outer layers are the crises of confidence and love. In this naked state the Christian hangs on to belief in God, for the only adequate reason – that he is God! But it is not *seen*, only blindly believed. By remaining 'faithful' through this ultimate testing, the Christian emerges with a deepened and more personal faith in the Father and the Son. Based on this faith, Christian hope gains strength, and all is set for the flowering of pure love in union with God. This is the goal of all Christian living and the sign that the divinisation of baptism is beginning to come true.

For the purposes of analysis we have dealt with the two crises of Christian life separately (in Chapter 13 and this chapter) as if they were distinct and successive. In actual fact no such division is possible, because both crises, that on the emotional-moral level and that on the personal-theological level, occur together. It is not possible to say that we emerge from one crisis and enter the next as if Christian development followed a geometric pattern. Often the crisis of faith comes before any crisis of morals, as many could testify today. The picture we are looking for is not therefore that of a rectilinear pattern like a track along which a person moves. It is more like a spiral in which we constantly travel over the same ground and go round the same circuit, but each time at a deeper level. The bottom of the spiral is death, the final crisis of the Christian life.

The impression must not be given that these purifications are spiritually select events happening in an arena called 'religion' apart from life. As we have had occasion to note many times in this book, religion and life are not separate, for religion only has meaning if it has to do with life. The purification of our faith, hope and charity are happenings which take place in the middle of our daily lives, in bread queues and supermarkets, offices and factories, recreational centres and homes. They have to do with what we are and what we do in those places. The serious Christian is the man who undertakes to play his part in society and is active in helping his fellows at work and relaxation, the sort of man who votes in his trade union or woman who bothers about her neighbours and their troubles. It is in and through these sorts of doings that God works to purify us. The trials of hope and faith are the trials of trade union business and work for the telephone Samaritans, the humdrum trials of being father and mother of a family. Through these events, and through the very ordinary knots and tangles we get ourselves into, God works to purify us. He draws us to him not by separating us from the world, but by uniting us to the ongoing activity of his Son within the world. For a few of us the arena of this work in the world is a monastery or convent, but it is work in the world nevertheless. The Risen Christ makes all things new not by miraculous interventions without the help of men, but through the everyday work of individuals who have the faith, trust and love necessary to do his work. The divinisation of baptism works to make a new race of human beings in the world, who have to undergo many trials and deaths in their following of Christ, but who should be remarkable not for extraordinary gifts (see Chapter 8) but for the faith, trust and love they show their neighbour. Showing this to their neighbour is the outward sign that their inner lives are filled with the presence of God.

This book began with a consideration of the presence of God in the world where he meets man. We have tried to analyse this meeting between man and God. At the end of the analysis let us remember that to define an ineffable thing like the meeting between God and man is inevitably to empty it of some of its mystery. It is essential, therefore, to conclude with the truth that the relationship between men and God is not analysable in human terms, because we men can only understand things by separating them. But God and men are not to be separated. God fills all. I exist and so do all men my brothers. God fills us. We are present and God is present, but it is one presence, not two.

SUGGESTED FURTHER READING

Part I.
On our knowledge of God:
V. White: *God The Unknown* (Harvill Press, 1956), chs 2 & 3.
V. Lossky: *The Mystical Theology of the Eastern Church* (James Clark, 1957), ch. 2.
J. Robinson: *Exploration into God* (S.C.M., 1967, p.b.)
(Various): *Spirituality For Today* (S.C.M., 1968, p.b.)

On Christ:
F. Durrwell: *In The Redeeming Christ* (Sheed and Ward, 1966, p.b.)
W. Grossouw: *In Christ* (Geoffrey Chapman, 1960, p.b.)
P. Wikenhauser: *Pauline Mysticism* (Herder-Nelson, 1960)

On Liturgy:
C. Davis: *Liturgy and Doctrine* (Sheed and Ward, 1960, p.b.)
A. Jones: *God's Living Word* (Geoffrey Chapman, 1961)
(Various): *Liturgy and the Word of God* (The Liturgical Press, 1958)

On Grace:
P. Fransen: *Divine Grace and Man* (New American Library, 1965, p.b.)

Part. II. On Christian love:
M. D'Arcy: *The Mind and Heart of Love* (Collins, 1954, p.b.)
Thérèse of Lisieux: *Autobiography of a Saint* (Collins, 1958, p.b.)
P. Teilhard de Chardin: *Le Milieu Divin* (Collins, 1965, p.b.)
G. Vann: *The Divine Pity* (Collins, 1960, p.b.)
Theo Westow: *Who Is My Brother?* (Sheed and Ward, 1966, p.b.)

Part III.
M. Buber: *I and Thou* (T. and T. Clark, 1959)
J. Goldbrunner: *Cure of Mind and Cure of Soul* (Burns Oates, 1958)
R. Haughton: *The Transformation of Man* (Geoffrey Chapman, 1967)
John of the Cross: *Ascent of Mt Carmel* and *Dark Night of the Soul* (Burns Oates, 1953)

APPENDIX

In Chapter 14 we described briefly a simple form of contemplative prayer. For those who are interested in reading more about it we append here a list of easy books for beginners. Although prayer is not primarily a technique, it nevertheless is also that. These books should help those who already have the desire to learn how to pray.

Anon: *The Cloud of Unknowing* (Penguin, 1961, p.b.)
L. Boase: *The Prayer of Faith* (Geoffrey Chapman, 1952)
A. Bloom: *Living Prayer* (D.L.T., 1966, p.b.)
E. Boylan: *Difficulties in Mental Prayer* (Gill and Son, 1967, p.b.)
C. Butler: *Prayer, Adventure in Living* (D.L.T., 1961, p.b.)
J. Chapman: *Spiritual Letters* (Sheed and Ward, 1961, p.b.)
R. Guardini: *Prayer in Practice* (Burns Oates, 1957)
J. N. Grou: *How To Pray* (James Clarke, 1955)
M. Hollings: *Hey You!* (Burns Oates, 1954, p.b.)
T. Merton: *Seeds of Contemplation* (Burns Oates, 1960, p.b.)
M. Quoist: *Prayers of Life* (Gill and Son, 1967, p.b.)
The Christian Response (Gill and Son, 1965, p.b.)
R. Steuart: *Map of Prayer* (Burns Oates, 1950, Paternoster Series)
D. Steere: *Dimensions of Prayer* (D.L.T., 1963, p.b.)
H. Van Zeller: *Choice of God* (Burns Oates, 1956)
R. Voillaume: *Seeds of the Desert* (Burns Oates, 1954)
Brothers of Men (D.L.T., 1963, p.b.)
O. Wyon: *Prayer* (Collins, 1962, p.b.)

INDEX

THEOLOGY TODAY SERIES

The following numbers *have already been published:*

No. 1	The Theology of the Incarnation	(Ralph Woodhall, S.J.)
No. 2	Theology and Revelation	(Gerald O'Collins, S.J.)
No. 3	The Theology of Faith	(John Coventry, S.J.)
No. 4	The Theology of the Trinity	(Laurence Cantwell, S.J.)
No. 5	The Theology of Creation	(Robert Butterworth, S.J.)
No. 7	The Theology of History	(Osmund Lewry, O.P.)
No. 8	The Theology of the Church	(Peter Hebblethwaite, S.J.)
No. 9	Theology of Ecumenism	(Michael Hurley, S.J.)

The following numbers will be published in *September 1970:*

No. 10	The Theology of Inspiration	(John Scullion, S.J.)
No. 12	The Theology of the Word of God	(Aloysius Church, S.J.)
No. 16	The Theology in St. Paul	(Henry Wansbrough, O.S.B.)
No. 18	Theology of Spirituality	(John Dalrymple)
No. 21	The Christian Social Conscience	(Rodger Charles, S.J.)
No. 25	The Theology of Baptism	(Lorna Brockett, R.S.C.J.)

First published in the Nederlands
Made and printed by Bosch, Utrecht